The Cradle of Quakerism

The Cradle of Quakerism:
Exploring Quaker Roots in North West England

by Arthur Kincaid

First published October 2011

Quaker Books, Friends House, 173 Euston Road, London NW1 2BJ.

www.quaker.org.uk

The moral rights of the author are asserted in accordance with the Copyright, Designs and Patents Act 1988. All rights reserved. No part of this book may be reproduced or utilised, in any form or by any means, electronic or mechanical, without permission in writing from the publisher. Reviewers may quote brief passages. Enquiries should be addressed to the Publications Manager, Quaker Books, Friends House, 173 Euston Road, London NW1 2BJ.

ISBN 978-1-907123-22-1

© Arthur Kincaid 2011

Cover image: Howgills from Firbank Fell.
Photo © Martin Lawrence 2011

All images supplied by www.martinlawrencephotography.com

Book designed and typeset by Cox Design, Witney

Printed by RAP Spiderweb, Oldham

Excerpt from "Little Gidding" Part 1 from *Four Quartets* copyright 1942 by T. S. Eliot and renewed 1970 by Esme Valerie Eliot, reprinted by permission of Houghton Mifflin Harcourt Publishing Company and Faber and Faber Ltd.

Excerpt from *The priory church of St Mary and St Michael* by Eric Rothwell reprinted by permission of the late Revd Canon Erick Rothwell of Cartmell.

Extracts from the Authorized Version of the Bible (The King James Bible), the rights of which are vested in the Crown, are reproduced by permission of the Crown's Patentee, Cambridge University Press.

While every effort has been made to contact copyright holders of material reproduced in this book, the publisher would be glad to rectify in future editions any errors or omissions.

CONTENTS LIST

	Preface	1
Chapter 1	Introduction	3
Chapter 2	1652: Brief summary of events	9
Chapter 3	Pendle Hill	15
Chapter 4	Yorkshire	19
Chapter 5	Brigflatts	25
Chapter 6	Preston Patrick and Yealand	35
Chapter 7	Kendal	45
Chapter 8	Swarthmoor	53
Chapter 9	Lancaster	65
Chapter 10	The Lake District	69
Chapter 11	Conclusion	77
Chapter 12	Further Reading	81
Chapter 13	Endnotes	85
Chapter 14	Bibliography	91

PREFACE

The birthplace of Quakerism: a handbook for the 1652 Country by Elfrida Vipont Foulds was published in 1952 for the tercentenary and reprinted several times. In 2009 a decision was made that rather than being reprinted again it should be rewritten. It is a daunting task to write a replacement for a book by a revered author, and I do not have her intimate knowledge of the area over a long period of time. I knew the upper part of the district well, but I have appreciated the opportunity to get to know the rest. I am immensely grateful to Brigflatts Meeting for short periods of quiet contemplation en route, and glad that it is able to be open much more of the time than are most places of worship now.

During my investigations I have tried to maintain an open mind about what seem to have become Quaker myths, and have not had time or expertise to investigate these fully. How large a community was Brigflatts? Did George Fox stay in this room or that? Was it really Firbank Fell where Fox preached, when a 1690 account says the chapel had been moved there "lately"? All I can do – feeling myths should not be perpetuated as history – is indicate where there may be controversy, and hope I have not started other myths.

As I travelled, the words that kept echoing in my mind as a theme for the journey were T. S. Eliot's from 'Little Gidding', where once, with a friend, I read *Four Quartets* aloud in the chapel:

> If you came this way,
> Taking any route, starting from anywhere,
> At any time or at any season,
> It would always be the same: you would have to put off
> Sense and notion. You are not here to verify,
> Instruct yourself, or inform curiosity
> Or carry report. You are here to kneel
> Where prayer has been valid.

I later found these lines have echoed similarly for other Friends.

I should like to thank the following for their kind assistance: Jennifer Armitage, David Boulton, Jenny Foot, Myra Ford, Hilary Hinds, Jim Jarvis, Alison Findlay, Pauline and Jon Nixon, Jenny Paull, James Postlethwaite, Tess Satchell, Bill Shaw, Robert Straughton, Roy Stephenson, Richard Taylor, Catherine Thomas, Meg Twycross, Alison Tyas, Jean Wangermann, the West Oxfordshire discussion group of Oxford Meeting, the farm couple who helped me change my tyre near Pardshaw, my wife Deirdre for letting me take the car away for 11 days, then for accompanying me and map reading on my final trip, and for proofreading, David Jones for his interest, encouragement and checking grid references (the scientific items are for him), and Angus Winchester for making invaluable suggestions and reading this in draft.

I have few qualifications for the task other than having been a Friend for 57 years, ten in a Friends' school, where I attended meeting for worship twice weekly and enjoyed a compulsory Quakerism course. What qualifications I have are due to my superlative teachers at Westtown School in Pennsylvania. To the Westtown family, past, present and future, I dedicate this book.

1

Introduction

The '1652 Country' is a name given by the Society of Friends (Quakers) to the part of England where in that year Quakers originally began to be drawn together. The area is roughly contained in the historical counties of northwestern Yorkshire, northern Lancashire and Westmorland (most now included in the county of Cumbria). It had its focus in Swarthmoor Hall, near Ulverston. Parts of it fall within the Lake District National Park. Many places in this area have given their names to American Quaker institutions – Swarthmore (a variant spelling) to a leading college, Pendle Hill to a study centre, Crosslands and Kendal to retirement communities.

The purpose of this book is to assist travellers, both Quakers and those interested in the cultural associations of landscape, in devising their own tours of the region. The chapters mainly follow Elfrida Vipont Foulds's groupings of several locations close to each other, but are more closely related to George Fox's travels. Most chapters also mention local places of interest not associated with 17th-century Quakerism. The book concludes with suggestions for further reading.

Travelling and staying in the area

This book describes the overall geography, routes and features, but updated information about travel, accommodation etc. will be found on the Britain Yearly Meeting website at www.quaker.org.uk/1652. The area is covered mostly by Ordnance Survey Landranger map 97 (Kendal & Morecambe, Windermere & Lancaster), but also 96 (Barrow-in-Furness & South Lakeland) and 103 (Clitheroe & Skipton). Some places otherwise difficult to find will be clear on these, and Ordnance Survey maps contain an explanation of how to follow grid references, which are used in this book: e.g. SD 282773 is the grid reference for Swarthmoor Hall.

Although the area is now well served by modern roads, going from place to place is sometimes time-consuming and difficult. Often routes are over or around mountains or have to avoid bodies of water. Travellers should be prepared for journeys to take a long time. Driving can be tiring, often on narrow, winding, hilly, sometimes single-lane roads. Views, though, particularly on mountain routes, may compensate for delay.

Public transport is not practical for getting around most of the area. A journey on foot is the only way of following anything like George Fox's route, so far as it can be ascertained. David and Anthea Boulton did this in 1994 and wrote about it. It took them two weeks.

Stout walking shoes (preferably fell boots), with soles that do not slip, are recommended if any walking is to be done: without such footwear, Pendle Hill is a risky walk. Travellers should bear in mind that even if they intend not to go far, walks sometimes extend themselves and weather is immensely changeable. One should never be without a waterproof jacket, even on the brightest, warmest day, and should always carry water. Kendal mint cake is a wonderful, portable local stamina-booster. Never walk without a map.

The area, earlier and now

Early in the 18th century Daniel Defoe described Westmorland as "a county eminent only for being the wildest, most barren and frightful of any that I have passed over in England". "Nor were these hills high and formidable only", he says, "but they had a kind of an unhospitable terror in them. . . . all barren and wild, of no use or advantage either to man or beast."[1] Such accounts surprise us today, since this area is now known as one of the most attractive in the world, with rivers, lakes and mountains, waterfalls and abundant walking trails. Not until the late 18th century was terror recognised as a significant aspect of beauty, of sublimity. The country is covered with fells, from the Old Norse 'fjall', meaning rocky upland; fell walking for pleasure came in with the influence of Coleridge and Wordsworth. People now have leisure to indulge in landscape for pastime. They did not in 1652.

At that time the country contained, as now, a fair amount of cultivated land and common pasture. It was sparsely populated by yeomen, who tended to farm their own land between the fells. Drovers' roads serving the cattle trade connected settlements. More people worked on farms then than do now. A township or settlement functioned collectively, but as J.D. Marshall puts it in *Old Lakeland*, "There is plenty of evidence that the Cumbrian *could* be an individualist. How else could southern Lakeland have been the cradle of that most radical of all religious creeds, Quakerism?".[2] The landscape was also distinguished by castles and strong gentlemen's houses to protect against raids from Scotland.

In the mid-19th century, Wordsworth's fame and the railways brought tourism, but it was a while before people came to explore the Quaker heritage. In 1905 John Wilhelm Rowntree suggested the attraction to "climb Pendle Hill with Fox and see once more his vision of 'a great people to be gathered'".[3] Ernest Taylor organised the first Quaker tours of the '1652 Country' around 1930.

My method has been to try to follow as far as possible George Fox's route, as documented in his *Journal*, joining in chapters places close enough to be seen in a day or sometimes two. Of course people will differ – some may wish to take it more slowly, others will prefer to go faster and skip some things: see www.quaker.org.uk/1652 for suggested itineraries.

The focus on George Fox is as "First Friend", a position justified by his inspirational personality and organisational ability, but other founders of the Quaker movement were his equals in early leadership. As well as Margaret Fell at Swarthmoor, some of the others appear in this book as I come to sites particularly associated with them. Fox dictated his *Journal* in 1674–75, well after the events depicted in it. The delay has sometimes caused confusion regarding his route.

A remarkable number of houses still exist which were intimately connected with early Quakerism. Most are still working farms or private homes, occupied by non-Friends. **Most of these people will not want to be disturbed and should not be**. It is usually possible to see the places easily from the outside.

2

1652: Brief summary of events

Civil war resulted in the execution of Charles I in 1649 and the assumption of power by Oliver Cromwell in 1653. The government of England was for the first time republican. For a short period after the war, people felt freer than ever before to think for themselves. Anglicanism had been abolished and the attempt to substitute Presbyterianism had not succeeded. Many felt church reform should accompany state reform. There was great urgency about it, since so radical a change in government led people to believe the Apocalypse was at hand: God must have overthrown the monarchy for a reason, and the world had quickly to be prepared for Jesus to return and rule it. The Bible had recently become readily available in English: people knew it well and quoted it regularly. Religion was a live issue.

The north, poor and isolated, had long been a place of sanctuary for Catholics, whose religion was outlawed. Sects abounded. The Separatists or Seekers were people who had left the organised church. As they grew aware of each other, they met together, sometimes to hear travelling ministers, sometimes to sit in silent waiting for God to declare himself. When a thought surfaced which seemed to have a divine source, an individual would speak. Though some, such as the Westmorland Seekers, were in coherent groups, others were widely scattered and needed focus.

George Fox was to draw together many of those in search of a new religious impetus. From a Leicestershire family of weavers, he became an itinerant minister between 1647 and 1650, moved northwards through Yorkshire, and from 1650 consolidated his ideas into a mission. The followers of the religious ideas he spread were called 'Quakers', originally a derogatory term, which some said came from the tendency of members to tremble when they spoke, but which Fox traced to Justice Bennet of Derbyshire who in 1650 "first called us 'Quakers' because we bid them tremble at the word of God".[1] In rural country people toiled hard and long on the land. The climate of the time was very cold, resulting in poor crops, and three bad harvests in succession meant poorer members of the populace nearly starved.

As he walked northward with Richard Farnsworth in the spring of 1652, Fox had fasted for several days when he felt God move him to climb to the top of Pendle Hill in Lancashire. The biblical associations of mountains would have been one reason that he was drawn there. To the local people, the area may have had an association with demonic powers: mountains were regarded as rough and forbidding, and also, not long before, the 'Pendle Witches' had been hanged for suspicious activities in the area.

Having struggled up the hill (see Chapter 3), Fox, looking westward as far as the sea, saw a region where the Lord "had a great people to be gathered" and was moved to "sound the day of the lord",[2] as in Joel 2:1–2: "Blow ye the trumpet to Zion, and sound an alarm in my holy mountain . . . for the day of the LORD cometh, for it is nigh at hand; . . . a great people and a strong; there hath not been ever the like, neither shall be any more after it, even to the years of many generations". Unlike the Fifth Monarchists, who tried to prepare for Christ's imminent second coming by destroying the government, Fox proclaimed spiritual rather than temporal reality: Christ was already here, and could teach his people himself. They had no need of "hireling priests" or "steeple-houses": they were themselves the church. They required no sacraments, which were only outward symbols of inward experience. Revelation was still occurring: every person had God within – not just men, not just university graduates – so anyone could minister. And through listening to that of God inside themselves, everyone could be saved – not just the Elect, as the dominant Calvinism would have it. This was a religion of personal experience, requiring no intermediaries. It was optimistic, focusing on love and mercy, not terrors and threats such as darkened the conventional approach to religion.

Although Friends now count pacifism as central to their beliefs, this testimony took several years to become truly part of Quakerism. At the time of founding it was the army which supplied Quakerism with crucial support. Cromwell had organised his New Model Army on the basis of its members' godliness. Soldiers were serious about religion, and radical religious thought flourished in the army, which was thought of as an instrument of God to punish earthly evil and usher in the kingdom of Jesus. Many prominent early Friends had been members of Cromwell's army.

After descending the hill, Fox began a progress through the hilly region further north, declaring his message, evidently following a local network of contacts associated with the New Model Army (see Chapter 4). He went on through the Yorkshire Dales to the home of Richard Robinson at Brigflatts on the Rawthey (Chapter 5), attended a large Separatist meeting at Borrats, and visited the neighbouring town of Sedbergh on the day of the hiring fair, convincing many. Moving west, he was invited to a Separatist meeting at Firbank Fell. Taking a position on or near the top of the rocky summit, he says he spoke for about three hours to around a thousand people.

He travelled through Westmorland (Chapter 6), and came to Preston Patrick, where he spoke to the monthly 'general meeting' of several hundred Separatists. He went on to Kendal (Chapter 7) and spoke in the town hall. Next he crossed Scout Scar to Underbarrow chapel, whose priest "fled away"; at Staveley-in-Cartmel the church warden threw him "headlong over a wall", one of many physical attacks in his years of preaching.

His most important stop was Swarthmoor Hall (Chapter 8), near Ulverston, the home of Thomas Fell, Judge of Assize and Chancellor of the Duchy of Lancaster, his wife Margaret, and their family of six daughters and one son. Judge Fell was well known for his hospitality to travelling ministers. But the parents were not at home, so, after a disputation with William Lampitt, the pastor of their church at Ulverston, Fox pressed on. He travelled back to some of the places he had previously visited and to new ones: Rampside, Walney Island, Gleaston, Dendron, Lancaster and Yealand, meeting Separatists and disputing with ministers. He spoke in chapels, private homes, alehouses and the open air.

In his subsequent travels, Fox kept coming back to Swarthmoor Hall, meeting and convincing Margaret Fell and her daughters and servants, and making an impression on Judge Fell, who allowed Friends to meet in his home and was clearly sympathetic to their beliefs, though his official position prevented his joining them. He later protected them from persecution. Margaret Fell, a born administrator, became Fox's equal in supporting the growing movement. He made Swarthmoor Hall his long-term base, and eleven years after Judge Fell died, he and Margaret Fell were married. They wrote pamphlets, kept in contact with the growing body of Friends, looked after them when imprisoned, and organised support for Quaker ministers who spread the movement south throughout England and to Ireland, to the chief population centres of London, Bristol and Norwich, to America, Jamaica, Holland and Germany. Although, following Ernest Taylor's book, these people are now referred to as the 'Valiant Sixty', there were closer to seventy. Fox's intention was clearly to gather about seventy ministers, on biblical precedent: in Luke 10:1–2 Jesus "appointed other seventy also, and sent them two and two . . . into every city and place whither he himself would come". Likewise those who spread Quakerism went in twos, visiting either places where Fox had already spoken or places he would later visit himself, so that the message was first given, then consolidated. Often the *Journal* speaks of how quickly a meeting was "settled" in a particular place.

Many early converts were agricultural workers, more of them yeomen than lower in the scale, and many were involved in crafts or trades, particularly associated with leather or cloth. Only a few, such as the Fells, and later William Penn, were gentry. Friends were strikingly literate and wrote many pamphlets and books. The preponderance of them were, like George Fox, young. Within a few years, their number had grown from a few hundred to as many as 40,000 or more as estimated by historians such as Barry Reay.[3]

3

Pendle Hill

We'll start the tour with Pendle Hill, where George Fox, looking northwest, had a vision of "a great people to be gathered". It must have been an unusually clear day, for he was able to see the Irish Sea from the top. By road it is reachable by the A682 from both directions. Fox is assumed to have gone up between Barley and Downham. Leaving Barley (SD 821406) on the road toward Downham, park on the left and take the route near Pendle Side Farm (SD 814416). Take the (signposted) track to the right of the farm. Go through the gate marked Pendle Hill Circular Walk. The path soon divides. Take the path to the right, which is stepped with large stones. Toward the top channels appear, to direct water down the hillside and help prevent erosion. This was a problem then as well: William Camden in the 16th century mentioned damage to the terrain caused by water running off Pendle Hill.

The hill is 1,827 feet (557 metres) above sea level, and about 690 ft (210 m) above Pendle Side Farm. Allow at least 30 minutes to get to the top. It is not a particularly arduous (or interesting) climb, but George Fox made it "with great ado": he had not eaten for several days. Perhaps he meant he was puffing by the time he arrived at the top. You will be too. Below is a tissue of farms with outlines of their dry stone walls, and in the distance the hills. Mist obscured any sight of sea both times I climbed, though the first was warm and sunny, at just the time of year Fox climbed.

On the way down, toward Downham, he drank from Deep Clough Spring, now sometimes called 'Fox's Well' or 'Robin Hood's Well'. Don't try to find this without a map called "Paths around Pendle", available locally. There is no record of where the alehouse was where Fox and Farnsworth spent the night afterwards, but there Fox had a vision of "a great people in white raiment by a river's side coming to the Lord",[1] echoing Revelation 3:5: "He that overcometh, the same shall be clothed in white raiment; and I will not blot out his name out of the book of life . . ."

Driving around the area one begins to understand the attraction of Pendle Hill and its association with witchcraft. It seems to dominate the landscape from every point and begins to feel magical, menacing or both. It has been a site of pagan worship from prehistoric times.

Go on via the A682 and A65, turning off onto the A683 for

Sedbergh or continuing on to the A590 for Kendal; alternatively the A59 towards Preston and then the M6 northwards can be quicker, if much less scenic.

Other places of interest
Downham (SD 785443), with a view of Pendle Hill, is one of the prettiest villages in the country, with stone houses and stocks on the village green bordered by a stream with ducks.
Grindleton (SD 760456), Rufus Jones's favoured location for the inn where Fox and Farnsworth stayed, is on the western side of the A59, after going through Chatburn. It is the place of origin of the Grindletonian sect, which anticipated Friends in many important respects. Go through it to get to:
Sawley (SD 778466), where the ruins of Sawley Abbey are worth seeing, with their view of Pendle Hill. Turn back toward Grindleton to find Sawley meeting house, since its sign can be spotted only in that direction. On the right shortly after the bridge over the Ribble, it's an attractive building, dating from 1777, with a lovely garden in front.
Barrowford Heritage Museum has three displays: on building techniques over the ages, on religions in the 17th century (Baptists, Quakers, Methodists, Catholics) and on the Pendle Witches.
Airton is a very beautiful grey stone village set in green hilly country. The meeting house (1700), on the village green, holds meeting for worship on alternate Sunday afternoons. Hostel accommodation is available in the former stable block.
Settle, between the Ribble and rocky hillside, has an active Quaker meeting in a building that dates from 1678, with a place for women's meetings in the balcony separated by partitions (see Brigflatts, p. 27).

4

Yorkshire

Dentdale – Wensleydale – Garsdale

George Fox's route through the Dales as described in his *Journal*, dictated long after the events described, is incomprehensible. Possibly he went through Skipton and Settle, north via the Ribble valley, and northeast along the old Roman road to Bainbridge. David Boulton suggests he then came over Cam Fell to Stonehouse.[1] Since we have no means of knowing, it is simplest to start from Sedbergh (SD 651920) and make a circular tour, starting with Dentdale. (This can be reversed if you wish.) Sedbergh, originally in Yorkshire, is described in the next chapter.

Dentdale
Entering Dentdale from Sedbergh down the road to Dent, one passes on the left a stone manor called Gate, once home to Alexander Hebblethwaite, an early Friend. When 17th-century people spoke of "Dent", they meant not just the town but the whole of the narrow dale, 11 miles (17.6 km) long. It is lush and unspoiled with the River Dee running through it.

The road through the small town of Dent (SD 705870) is narrow and twisting, turning up and down hill, with houses fitting in as they can, some picturesquely quirky. If you meet a wide vehicle driving through Dentdale you may have to back up quite a distance, for passing places are infrequent.

The Separatists or Seekers in the north were described in *The first publishers of truth* as "A religious people separated from the Common Nationell Worshippe",[2] and were closely connected with each other. There was evidently an efficient and speedy means of circulating handwritten copies of pamphlets as well as letters (indeed Fox was writing and having something copied for circulation at his inn after climbing Pendle Hill).

In the north there had been a long tradition of independence. Parishes were large, and chapels of ease were sometimes served by readers appointed by the community. David Boulton surmises that where ministers were absent, congregations might stay together with a lay ministry, and these were the people most susceptible to Quakerism.[3]

"In the year 1652 came George Fox to Stonehouses in Dent...".[4] Stonehouse Farm (SD 771858) appears at the head of a road off to the left marked as a T junction, a short way after the road passes the Sportsmans Inn on the right and crosses a bridge. Probably part of the main house and the barn are original. The farmhouse, home to one of the leaders of the local tithe strike, later became a meeting house. Tithe resistance was common to the radical movements of the time, and in April 1652 tenants of Dent and Garsdale banded together to withhold tithes.[5] That money from the annual assessment went to Trinity College, Cambridge is an example of how iniquitous the system – supposed to provide sustenance for the local vicar – had become.

Though enlightened in one way, the denizens of Dentdale were not immediately drawn to Fox's message: "a company of great professors in the Independent way . . . being rich & full of knowledge in their own Conseit were not sensible of want of information".[6] The convincement of people in this area took the later efforts of Richard Hubberthorne and Richard Robinson of Countersett (not the same as Richard Robinson of Brigflatts).

Dentdale had two meeting houses: one known as Loneing in Dent itself (SD 703871), no longer standing, and the other further up the Dale at Lea Yeat, built 1702 (SD 761869), now a private house, River View, in Cowgill. Meetings were sometimes held in other houses beyond Dent, some of which still stand.

After the railway bridge the landscape opens out, and you find yourself on a hilltop. On either side stretch plains of scrubby vegetation cropped by sheep.

Wensleydale

Turn left to Hawes (SD 874898), 7 miles (11 km) along the B6255. You are now in Wensleydale. In Hawes is a small Friends' burial ground (1680–1943), near the Hawes Ropemakers. The Hawes meeting house (1710) was demolished in 1955.

Take the A684 eastwards, in the direction of Aysgarth and Leyburn. You are now on a clear open road with soft green grass and trees. Coming into Bainbridge (SD 934903), just as you turn left toward Askrigg you find on the right a Friends' meeting house, built in 1836 (the original, in another location, was founded in 1669). There are gravestones in the tall grass on both sides. At the time of writing, meeting for worship is held here each Sunday except the last Sunday of the month, when it is at Countersett.

Go on to Askrigg (SD 948910), a place of brownish stone. It was the market town of Wensleydale when George Fox visited on market day: he had "not much persecution"[7] when he spoke in the "steeplehouse" after the priest had finished. The church, St Oswald's, is mediaeval, with a crenellated tower and very attractive interior. It was presumably somewhere near Askrigg that he was locked up in "a great house where there was a schoolmaster", on the assumption that "I was a young man that was mad and was got away from my relations". He was let out because of the sanity of his answers "and the Truth I spoke to them".[8] Go back to Bainbridge and take the road marked Semerwater and Countersett (SD 919879). Countersett Hall is a private home with beautiful garden. Here lived Richard Robinson, gentleman farmer, educated, "but not at the Universities";[9] he was away and missed Fox's visit to Countersett. He had "been under Deep Travell of Spirit after ye Substance of Religon some years before, & hearing (at a Distance) what G. ffox Preached for Doctrine, he joined with it in his mind"[10] and went to meetings of Fox's followers at Todthorne in Grayrigg, Francis Howgill's home, then, with his friend Thomas Taylor, minister of Preston Patrick, to one at Hutton, where he was convinced. When in 1652 Richard Hubberthorne came to Countersett Hall, Robinson left home and joined him on a mission through Wensleydale. Later they were imprisoned in York Castle. While Robinson pursued a career as itinerant minister through the north, Countersett Hall was the principal meeting place for Quakers in the Dales. George Fox visited it in 1677. Richard Robinson's son Michael later built a new meeting house in the village, adapting it from a barn. Some parts which survived the rebuilding of 1778 are in the present lovely meeting house, still used for worship monthly (see Bainbridge). The tiny former schoolhouse is now a cottage in front of it.

Semerwater (SD 920870) is reached by a very steep hill. The legend is that a town was submerged there, and Bronze Age remains have been found when the level is low. The level was unusually low when I saw it, so if one were ever to see evidences of occupation submerged in it, surely it would have been that day, but I saw nothing. The bridge over the river was contributed by local Friends in 1770.

You may want to carry along the road from Countersett Hall past Semerwater and see Carr End (SD 929869), where the Fothergill family lived, of which one was Dr John Fothergill, eminent scientist and founder of Ackworth School.

Garsdale

Fox went on to Garsdale, met Major Bousfield and other "great professors"[11] and had little success. There was a meeting house at Garsdale from 1703 until 1900, demolished 1912. Go back to Hawes, pass through it again and take the A684 toward Sedbergh.

Other places of interest

Farfield Mill, on the A684 Garsdale to Hawes road, 1 mile (1.3 km) from Sedbergh, is a working textile mill, rescued from dereliction as an arts and heritage centre, with exhibitions about local weaving – always a leading craft here – arts and crafts galleries, a shop and café.

Hawes: Wensleydale cheese shop and museum.

Middleham has a splendid castle, where Richard III grew up and which he later owned in right of his wife.

Richmond is home to an original Georgian theatre, which still operates and is well worth seeing even if not in action.

5

Brigflatts

Brigflatts – Sedbergh – Draw-well – Firbank Fell – Cross Keys – Appleby

Sedbergh is the main centre for this part, but the historical focus inevitably starts at Brigflatts.

Brigflatts

Brigflatts (SD 641912) is a little way outside Sedbergh, off the A683. If you are taking the road north from Kirkby Lonsdale, the turning is on the right after the sign indicating you're entering Sedbergh; if coming from Sedbergh it is on the left shortly before leaving its environs. George Fox must have been given as a contact the name of one Richard Robinson of Brigflatts on the River Rawthey, and at Sedbergh sought directions to his home. Asked where he came from he answered confidently, "From the Lord".[1] Robinson put him up for the night, but had a moment of panic in the morning, fearing his guest might be a thief, and locked him in. Though it cannot be visited, Robinson's farmhouse is still standing, at the end of Brigflatts Lane, straight on past the meeting house. The room where Fox stayed is the one with the small square upstairs window on the left of the house.

The next morning Robinson and Fox went to a meeting at the nearby home of Gervase Benson. Formerly a colonel in the Commonwealth army, Benson, who had been mayor of Kendal, was a Justice of the Peace. He farmed Borrat and his wife's farm, Haygarth (now the Cross Keys Temperance Inn – see below). Later he lost his position for wishing to acquit James Nayler on trial in Appleby (see below). At Borrat Fox found "a mighty meeting",[2] including Separatists from areas "extending eastward down Swaledale and Wensleydale and westward to Preston Patrick and Yealand".[3] Several at that meeting were convinced, including Richard Robinson and his wife Mary, Thomas Blaykling, his son John and their wives Ann and Elinor.

If you follow the path labelled "to Birks" on the left near the start of Brigflatts Lane, go across the fields, under a railway bridge and a little further on, the white house across the road is Borret Farm (SD 645916), once Borrat or Borratts. By road, it is the second house on the right after turning down the A683 toward Kirkby Lonsdale from the A684. It has been modernised, the front rendered, with modern windows, and the sides have been painted, though you can see the stone underneath. On the opposite side of the road are the farm's barns, contemporary with the house.

Following Fox's preaching in Sedbergh and on Firbank Fell (see below), so many people were convinced locally that a meeting was "settled" in the Sedbergh area immediately. George Whitehead, one of the youngest of early Friends, who lived to a considerable age, recollected that "Our Meetings in Sedbergh then were often at Thomas Blaykling's House . . . and at Gervas Benson's House . . . at Richard Robinson's at Brigflats . . . and at other Places near . . .".[4] Regular large gatherings for business of Friends from scattered localities occasioned need for larger accommodation which was not open to the elements. There may have been a legal consideration too: when Friends met in private houses the owner was liable for permitting an illegal assembly.

In 1660 Friends purchased part of Richard Robinson's orchard for a burial ground. A stable was built next to it. The meeting house at Brigflatts, earlier known as Sedbergh Meeting, is the oldest purpose-built meeting house in the north (the oldest are Hertford, 1670, and Alton in Hampshire, 1672). The ground was bought in 1674: it had been owned by Robinson, but by then he was himself in the graveyard. The meeting house was in use the following year. It is long and thin, with windows only at the front. A balcony on two sides was added later. Most meeting houses eventually had a separate area for the women's meeting – which did not indicate separation at times of worship but that women had separate meetings for their own particular business, mainly concerned with helping the poor. In this meeting, as at Swarthmoor, these were in loft space, separated by a partition that could be raised and lowered. At Brigflatts this area was eventually converted for a warden's flat.

Friends' meeting houses are a unique form of ecclesiastical building. The basis was probably barn or cottage architecture. A "minister's stand" – raised facing benches with a panel of wood behind them, where registered ministers and "weighty Friends" would sit – was usually included in those built before the 20th century. Egalitarian for their time, Friends' meetings have gradually become more so. Whereas in my childhood "weighty Friends" still sat on the facing benches, and their ministry tended to be somewhat pontifically intoned, seating now tends to be in a circle or square formation. "Weighty Friends" are not so easily distinguished now, and messages are conversational in style and tone.

Many meeting houses doubled as schools, since Friends chose to educate their children themselves. They would wish to avoid the schools of the established church, which would probably exclude their children anyway. Many early Friends left money for education. Brigflatts Meeting built a schoolhouse above an extension to the stable, now used for the children's meeting on Sundays.

George Fox claimed that he recognised in Brigflatts the manifestation of his vision of people in white raiment. This is open to interpretation. The traditional explanation is that Brigflatts was at the time a large community of flax workers, although the local historical society is unaware of any evidence for a multitude of flax workers at Brigflatts. David Boulton says that the community was very small: Sedbergh parish registers show only three families in Brigflatts during the first half of the 17th century.[5] Nor do the meeting's burial records indicate a large community. Nevertheless, Seekers came from the whole surrounding countryside, and at Whitsun might have been wearing white.

Brigflatts is a wonderful oasis for visitors who pass on walks or stop for quiet. It is both magical and very active, with the warden kept very busy talking to groups of visitors and school parties. In the graveyard lie Thomas Blaykling with his children John and Ann, and also the 20th-century poet Basil Bunting, whose most famous poem *Briggflatts* (spelt thus) was inspired by this place. Brigflatts is clearly a place "where prayer has been valid".

Sedbergh

Sedbergh (SD 651920), now just on the Cumbria side of the Yorkshire-Cumbria border, was in 1652 in one of the poorest and remotest districts of England, where religious radicalism was rampant. It is the site of a school founded in 1525, already famous in Fox's time. The town has recently been gaining fame and tourists as a book centre.

Having spent the night at Borrat (see below), on Wednesday, 9 June Fox attended the Whitsun hiring fair at Sedbergh. He preached through the fair, then spoke under a yew tree in the garth of St Andrew's Church. A piece of the yew tree can be seen on request at Brigflatts (though early Friends would have been dubious about this interest in relics!) .

Draw-well

George Fox went home with Thomas Blaykling and his son John to their farm at Draw-well (SD 634936). To get there today, take the road out of Sedbergh (on the left coming from Brigflatts) toward Howgill about 2 miles (3.2 km) north. Look carefully to the left for a sign engraved on a plaque in the stone wall saying "Bramaskew", at the entrance to a drive. This is the name of the farm, which at the time of writing offers bed and breakfast and also has self-catering accommodation in Drawell Cottage (so spelled today), a whitewashed cottage with a stone porch. You can get a good view of Drawell from the road: it is a white house with a long stone barn at the same roof height and pitch attached to its right.

George Fox is supposed to have slept in the smallest room upstairs, or according to another account he hid there to escape persecution from government troops. However, David Boulton points out[6] that Fox was not in the habit of fleeing, and the New Model Army tended to protect rather than to persecute Quakers. This room is only about 4 feet (1.3 m) square and is in a later extension to the house, as is plainly seen from the photograph. The owner suggested to me that, as with other houses of the period, the upstairs was not divided into rooms at the time of Fox's visit.

In 1665, Drawell was home to the "uninterrupted meeting", when a Friends' meeting was raided by militia. The manuscript *Great Book of Sufferings* in Friends House says "They drove the said People in fury & haste, Men, Women and Children (not suffering the said John Blaikling's wife in their own House to take her Hatt)".[7] The Friends were released, since no one knew what to do with them, and went back and resumed their meeting.

Drawell features again in 1676, when Friends met to discuss the Wilkinson–Story controversy. John Wilkinson and John Story challenged George Fox's leadership and methods for organising the Society of Friends. They worried that individual Light was being subordinated to the sense of the meeting. H. Larry Ingle and David Boulton picture the crowd of Friends in heated discussions in the house,[8] but according to others the discussion took place in the barn, which would surely better have accommodated so significant a gathering. Wherever it occurred, its solution, in the words of Christopher Hill, "meant an end to the absolute individualism in which the spirit of God led each Friend independently".[9] Still, it was only by exercising some standards of uniformity and control that the movement survived, alone of the radical sects of the time.

Firbank Fell

On Sunday 13 June there was to be a huge gathering of Seekers at Firbank Fell (SD 619937). Leading ministers Francis Howgill and John Audland were to speak. One can walk from Drawell to Firbank Fell today via the Dales Way, crossing the Lune to what was then its Westmorland side. Firbank Fell is on an unmarked road off the A684 (Sedbergh–Kendal) almost opposite where the B6256 goes south towards Middleton and Kirkby Lonsdale. Stone walls define the entrance to the road. (Do not go down the road marked "Firbank" nearer Sedbergh, which goes not to the fell but the village of that name.) Go 1¼ mile (2 km) up this narrow, winding road and over one cattle grid. Park opposite the second cattle grid and walk a bit forward. Firbank Fell is on the right.

Firbank Fell stood next to a chapel which Seekers had taken over for their meetings. To the right of the fell is a small paddock enclosed by stone walls. There is no sign of a church apart from a few gravestones level with the ground. A few trees are planted round the perimeter, and horses sometimes graze in the paddock. A plaque now on the rock, placed there for the tercentenary celebrations in 1952, says:

> LET YOUR LIVES SPEAK
> HERE OR NEAR THIS ROCK GEORGE FOX PREACHED
> TO ABOUT ONE THOUSAND SEEKERS FOR ABOUT THREE
> HOURS ON SUNDAY JUNE 13 1652. GREAT POWER
> INSPIRED HIS MESSAGE AND THE MEETING PROVED
> OF FIRST IMPORTANCE IN GATHERING THE SOCIETY
> OF FRIENDS KNOWN AS QUAKERS. MANY MEN AND
> WOMEN CONVINCED OF THE TRUTH ON THIS FELL AND
> IN OTHER PARTS OF THE NORTHERN COUNTIES WENT
> THROUGH THE LAND AND OVER THE SEAS WITH

THE LIVING WORD OF THE LORD ENDURING GREAT HARDSHIPS AND WINNING MULTITUDES TO CHRIST.
JUNE 1952

If you go behind the rock with the plaque on it, you'll find a natural amphitheatre. Fox seems likely to have spoken here, with his back to the church and the road. The voice gets lost if you face front but speaking back is cushioned by the terrain.

Some doubt has been cast on this location in that Thomas Machell, Rector of Kirkby Thore, recorded in his antiquarian notes as he travelled in 1692 that the chapel had been moved "lately" from nearer Killington, due to a land dispute.[10] Machell relied on an informant, and what "lately" would have meant must have depended on his age.

After Howgill and Audland preached in the chapel in the morning, Fox gave notice of an afternoon meeting. People went away for lunch; many returned. He was expected to speak in the chapel, but "the word of the Lord came to me that I must go and set down upon the rock in this mountain even as Christ had done before",[11] so he stood or sat on the rock, facing a "congregation" of around a thousand, as he records, who stood below him. This momentous meeting, in which Fox united the Yorkshire and Westmorland Seekers under his understanding of religion, has been regarded as the signal event in the founding of Quakerism.

There is an annual Firbank gathering on or near 13 June, although it may be diverted to Brigflatts in bad weather.

Cross Keys

Cross Keys Temperance Inn (SD 697968) was High Haygarth, a farm belonging to Dorothy Benson, Gervase Benson's wife. Its earliest record dates it to 1619, the later date on the front reflecting later owners. To get there go through Sedbergh and turn left onto the A683 toward Kirkby Stephen and Brough. The Inn is about 7 miles (11 km) along this road. There is a flat meadow behind it, then mountains sweep upward. In 1653 Dorothy Benson gave birth to her son, Emmanuel, while she was imprisoned in York,[12] having been arrested with Ann Blaykling from Drawell Farm for interrupting a church service. She died a year later and was buried in the garden here.

You can take the pleasant walk to the dramatic waterfall of Cautley Spout (about an hour, steepish only toward the end) from just to the right of the Inn. The area was home to Iron Age settlers.

Other Quaker sites in the Ravenstonedale area
There are several other places of former Quaker activity around Ravenstonedale that the enthusiast can follow up from David Butler's book on Quaker meeting houses, but they may be hard to find and have little to show.

Appleby
From the Cross Keys at Haygarth on the A683, Appleby (NY 695205) can be reached via Kirkby Stephen on the A685 and A66, or go left on the A685 past Ravenstonedale toward Tebay, then take the B6260 toward Orton and Appleby, an attractive town bisected by the River Eden. This is high, open country with sheep and rolling hills. Appleby, once the chief town of the region, suffered considerably from Scots raids, and so had a castle, but was otherwise underpopulated. Camden in the 16th century considered it "would be little better than a village" but for the importance of the assizes and prison in the castle.[13]

Appleby's association with Quaker history is the imprisonment there of Francis Howgill and James Nayler. A remarkable and controversial early Friend, Nayler in his writing shows great depth and inspiration. A Yorkshireman, he had been quartermaster under Major-General Lambert and was convinced as a Friend in 1651. Returning to his farm, he heard a voice telling him to leave everything and take to the road. He followed its insistence, and while early in the movement he was at least Fox's equal in inspiration and leadership, subsequent events led to his contribution being played down. During his early ministry in Orton and Appleby in 1653 he and Francis Howgill were arrested for blasphemy, because they claimed God was in them. What they referred to was "the Inner Light", that aspect of divinity Friends believe each of us carries, which it is one's responsibility to listen to and cultivate.

Nayler sometimes travelled with Fox. Eventually he went to

London to spread the message and there, exhausted by overwork and fasting, he allowed himself to be led by a fanatical group who idolised him. The outcome was that in 1656 he entered Bristol on horseback re-enacting Christ's entry into Jerusalem. He repeatedly stated that he did this "as a sign" of Christ's second coming, not imagining himself to be Christ except insofar as Christ resides in every human spirit. In Nayler's time such a re-enactment was considered blasphemous. Parliament was alarmed by Quakerism as "an organized movement which, from its base in the North, had swept with frightening rapidity over the southern counties"[14] and Nayler was their scapegoat. Many argued for his death, and his final sentence was just short of that. He was branded, his tongue bored through, and he was stocked and whipped in London and Bristol and imprisoned indefinitely. Released nearly three years later, he was physically broken, but his mind was very clear. He repented the damage he had done the movement, was reconciled with Fox, who had not treated him with any kindness or forbearance, and at the end of his life the most moving testimony is attributed to him, which begins: "There is a spirit which I feel that delights to do no evil, nor to avenge any wrong, but delights to endure all things, in hope to enjoy its own in the end. Its hope is to outlive all wrath and contention, and to weary out all exaltation and cruelty, or whatever is of a nature contrary to itself".[15]

Appleby Castle is not currently open. It is presumed to be Nayler's jail, but David Neelon in his book on Nayler feels that Howgill and Nayler may have been imprisoned in what he calls "The Armorer's House",[16] locally known as 'The Armoury'. It has now been modernised, has brown windows, and is called 'The Old Smithy'.

Francis Howgill, who went with Edward Burrough to establish Quakerism in London, was imprisoned again in Appleby and died there in 1668. He had been educated for the Anglican ministry but, dissatisfied with the superstition, became an Independent teacher, then tried the Baptists, finally accepted Quakerism and became a leading Quaker minister. He was buried at a farm called Sunny Bank to the east of his home village of Grayrigg, near Kendal, but the site of the grave is uncertain.

Pendle Hill from Great Mitton Bridge

Pendle Hill from Downham

Brigflats Meeting House

Brigflatts Meeting House

Brigflatts Quaker Burial Ground

ABOVE: Original Yew tree. BELOW: St. Andrew's Church

Drawell

ABOVE: Firbank Fell – Fox's Pulpit. BELOW: Firbank Fell amphitheatre

Preston Patrick

Yealand Meeting House

Swarthmoor Hall

Rampside and Peel Island

View from Sunbrick Quaker Burial Ground

Lancaster Castle and (below) dungeons

Colthouse Quaker Burial Ground

6

Preston Patrick and Yeland

*Crosslands – Low Park Farm – Preston Patrick – Camsgill –
Arnside and Silverdale – Yealand villages – Over Kellet – Halton*

Crosslands

If you are following George Fox's route as far as possible by road, go from Firbank Fell through Killington (SD 614889) and Old Hutton (SD 565885), then continue along the B6254 toward Kirkby Lonsdale until you see a sign for Gatebeck to the right. At the turn you will see Crosslands Farm (SD 571865), where Fox spent the night with John Audland, one of the Separatist ministers who had just been convinced at the felltop gathering, and his wife Ann. Nearby hamlets echo their surname. Crosslands, a working cattle farm, is on both sides of the road.

John Story, from nearby Goose Green, invited Fox to share a pipe. Fox, a non-smoker, worried that Story would think he "had not unity with the creation" if he refused, put the pipe in his mouth and gave it back again. Story he describes as having "a flashy, empty notion of religion".[1] David Boulton explains that the Ranters – who believed everything was acceptable – saw God in all things, animate and inanimate, and suggests Fox told the tale to undermine Story, who was to become a Friend and later would challenge his authority.[2] John Wilkinson came from Millholme, about 3 miles (2 km) further north near New Hutton (see Drawell, p. 30, on the "Wilkinson–Story" controversy).

From Crosslands, go down the hill, turn left and drive through Gatebeck.

Low Park Farm

Breaking the chronology of George Fox's period for a moment, you may want to make a slight diversion between Gatebeck and Preston Patrick to Low Park Farm (SD 541864), where John Woolman, the 18th-century American Quaker and anti-slavery campaigner, stayed in 1772. Turn right at the crossroads down Gatebeck Lane (not marked at this point), where there are signs to Kendal (A65) and Motorway (M6). Then turn right on Low Park Lane. The farm is on the right.

While staying with George and Jane Crosfield at Low Park, John Woolman wrote down his dream from two-and-a-half years before, in which he saw a gloomy mass of matter identified as human beings, with whom he was mixed up, "and that I might not consider myself as a distinct or separate being". He heard an angelic voice telling him that "John Woolman is dead",[3] which he ultimately understands to refer to the death of his own will. After writing this, he walked on by Kendal and Grayrigg, went to meeting at Countersett, and on to York where, soon after his arrival, he died of smallpox.

The little Quaker burial ground (SD 539865) known as Birkrigg Park (not to be confused with the residence of that name further along Low Park Lane) is close by along a footpath west towards Summerlands. It is marked on the Ordnance Survey 'Explorer' map (1:25,000 scale) but not the 'Landranger' (1:50,000). Here John Camm, John Audland and other early Friends were buried; the only stone is that of Anne Cartmell of Wath Sutton. Mabel Camm does not lie here. She long survived her husband John, who died in 1656, worn out with travel and exposure; she later married, as his second wife, Gervase Benson, who died in 1679. According to *The first publishers of truth*, Mabel Benson "continued a faithful and sencable woman to her end"[4] and at 87 was the first to be buried at Preston Patrick meeting house.

Going back down Low Park Lane, turn left, and right at the crossroads, continuing along the road that came through Gatebeck.

Preston Patrick

After Gatebeck and Goose Green (unmarked), you will pass the Preston Patrick meeting house complex on your right. Built in 1691, this small meeting house was almost completely rebuilt in 1869; worship still takes place there on Sundays. The burial ground is in front of it, with stones sunk in the ground. The stables and coach house, which had classrooms above, were built in 1869. This building and the former caretaker's cottage are now let.

Continuing down the narrow road, the first left turn leads to Preston Patrick Hall (SD 544838). There is a sign pointing toward the meeting house at the head of this drive, and if you turn left there you will see on a large stone the name of the hall. This is another working farm. Its treasure is the court room on its right-hand side. It is now reached by a very steep spiral staircase indoors, as well as from outdoors. This is where the law court was held in which many early Quakers were fined for non-payment of tithes. In adulthood,

Thomas Camm (see below) was a relentless tithe resister, suffered distraint of his goods 33 times and over 27 years paid the huge total of £62 12s 8d in fines. The hall, built in the late 14th century, was remodelled in the 15th and 16th, the beautiful tracery of the windows added in one of the renovations. In the hall is kept a walking stick once belonging to Robert Foster, a 19th-century Friend Wordsworth and Coleridge knew.

The name 'Preston Patrick' is from 'priest's town' and the name of an early owner of the great hall, Patrick de Culwen. In the 12th century there was briefly a monastic house there. In Fox's time it had become a regional centre for Separatist activity: he and Audland were to attend a Separatist General Meeting which met there monthly. This is particularly striking in view of the importance of the regular business meeting in the structure of the Society of Friends, until recently called the 'monthly meeting'. George Fox, a brilliantly inspired administrator, picked up ideas where he found them. People came to the meeting from Sedbergh, Yealand, Kellet, Kendal, Underbarrow, Grayrigg and Old Hutton.[5]

Preston Patrick's scattered parishioners had gained the right to nominate their own minister. Until recently this had been Thomas Taylor, a university-educated man who gave up his pulpit and moved away because he thought tithing was wrong. (He later became a Friend.) Now Francis Howgill and John Audland were the leaders of this group. On this occassion, Wednesday 16 June 1652, Fox was urged to address the meeting from the pulpit, but he insisted on taking a position near the door. After a long silence, during which Howgill several times opened his bible and almost spoke, George Fox preached to the gathering of several hundred. Thomas Camm, the son of Fox's host-to-be, was in the assembly and never forgot the occasion:

> After the said silence and waiteing, G.F. stood up in the mighty power of God, & in ye demonstration thereof was his mouth opened to preach Christ Jesus, the Light of life, & the way to God, & Saviour of all that beleive and obay him, which was delivred in that power and Authority that most of the Auditory, wch were sevrall hundreds, were Effectually

reached to the heart, & Convinced of the truth that very day, for it was the day of God's powr.

A notable day Indeed never to be forgotten by me, Thomas Cam . . . I being then present at that meeting. A schoole boy but aboute 12 years of age . . . do still remember that blessed and gloryouse day . . .[6]

Camsgill
On 17 or 18 June, Fox went on to stay at Camsgill (SD 548835), the house of husbandman John Camm and his wife Mabel (their serving maids Jane and Dorothy Waugh also became members of the 'Valiant Sixty'). This house is still standing, awkwardly reached from Preston Patrick Hall by going under the motorway. Park at the meeting house (or at the Hall, if you have permission) and walk; or drive on straight ahead, under the motorway. You'll see a sign saying Camsgill on your right. If you've driven, park beside the road a bit further along and walk up the drive. On your right is a "deep romantic chasm" called Hellgill, with a stream at the bottom. There are wild flowers and bracken near the road, woods down below. Local Friends used it secretly for meetings after the Conventicle Act of 1670 made dissenting gatherings illegal – though most gloried in continuing to meet openly. The motorway noise, acute at the entrance, fades as you walk up the drive, but the farm and stone barn are not available for close-up inspection.

Drive back to the road where Preston Patrick meeting house is, and go left. At the corner to your right is the Old School Gallery and Tea Room. If you enter its car park and look straight ahead you will see the parish church on a hill. This later building occupies the site of the one where Fox preached.

Arnside and Silverdale
From Preston Patrick turn right at the A6070, and after a short distance turn left at the Crooklands Hotel onto the B6385 to Milnthorpe. In Milnthorpe turn right to Arnside (SD 455785), a village overlooking the Kent estuary. Fox performed a healing here. Turn left for Silverdale (SD 460750), reached by a drive over

the hills, where Fox had "a great meeting of Friends" and was threatened by a priest "under a pretence to light a pipe of tobacco, but his intent was to have done a mischief with his pistol to me":

> The maid told her master and he clapped his hands a both sides the doorposts and told him he should not come in there, and looking up he spied a great company of men over the wall, one with a musket and others with stakes. But the Lord God prevented their bloody design, that they went their ways and did no harm.[7]

Yealand

Take the road toward Carnforth, and you will come to Yealand Redmayne (SD 501755), one of three Yealands, Storrs and Conyers being the other two. They lie on the ridge of a rocky hill, once a peninsula surrounded by sea and marsh, but now, as in 1652, surrounded by fields.

Yealand Redmayne, on high ground, was the home of Richard Hubberthorne, one of the early leaders of the Society of Friends, born in 1628. He had been a captain in the Commonwealth army. According to his colleague Edward Burrough, he was small of stature and weak in constitution, ". . . a good Companion in all conditions . . . He was a man of peace, and loved it, and walked peaceably among his brethren in honest, kind familiarity."[8] Hubberthorne was imprisoned in Newgate and died of prison fever (another term for typhus) at 34. A clock on the old schoolhouse in Yealand Conyers commemorates him.

Drive on and climb somewhat higher to Yealand Conyers (SD 504745), once home to the Quaker author Elfrida Vipont Foulds. Near the top of the hill look for a mounting block on the left-hand side of the road. The old schoolhouse, now used as a hostel, fronts the road. Behind it is the former headmaster's house, where the warden lives now, across from which is the meeting house. On three sides of it is the burial ground, which overlooks, down the hill, fields that belonged to 17th-century Friends. There are benches around it and a splendid big old beech tree in one corner. This has been a steady Quaker meeting, helped by the attraction of the area for retirement. People who attended Yealand Manor

School, for evacuee and refugee children during the Second World War, have come back to live here.

Many will find the Meeting House welcoming, with soft blue cushions on the benches in rows on three sides, and a long bench in 'front', with minister's stand behind it. A balcony is reached by stairs outside the meeting room. The porch displays the date 1692, but severe damage occurred in a 1737 fire to the thatched roof, after which it was largely rebuilt, and two sash windows replaced the mullioned ones. The old wall can be seen from outside, extended toward the roof, which has been rebuilt in slate.

Leighton Hall, near Yealand Conyers, was owned in 1652 by Sir George Middleton, a Catholic recusant. Suffering from fines levied on him, he tried to recover his losses by huge levies on his tenants, who took legal action. Some of these were farmers in the Yealands who became Friends. Both Middleton and Robert Bindloss of nearby Borwick Hall abused Friends as they went to and from Yealand Meeting. The road to Leighton Hall (SD 494744) is almost opposite the old schoolhouse in Yealand Conyers. The house, rebuilt since the 1650s, is the home of the Gillow family, in the luxury furniture trade from 1730 and later part of Waring & Gillow, so the tour concerns itself mostly with furnishings. The grounds and views are gorgeous.

Following signs from Yealand Conyers to Borwick, you will see Borwick Hall (SD 528730). The impressive hall and grounds are now used for outdoor activities programmes, but are not otherwise open to the public. It was the home of Sir Robert Bindloss, who sent his servants in disguise to attack Fox at Capernwray, where he had been attending a meeting in the house of Thomas Leaper. They broke up the meeting, thrusting about with their swords until the people had to snatch up chairs to protect themselves, and then searched the house, only to find that Fox had left some time before.[9]

The two disused burial grounds at Hilderstone (SD 518766) described by Butler,[10] are to the east of Yealand Redmayne, on the opposite side of the main road, down a lane turning to the left from the road to Burton and running parallel to the railway.

Over Kellet and Halton

Follow the sign to Over Kellet (SD 521699). When you get there, park and face the post office. Walk to your right along the road until you see on your left Brookside, now two houses, Brookside and Brookside Cottage: the latter shows more original features. This was the home of Robert Widders (or Withers), who accompanied Fox to America. Margaret Fell said of him:

> He was a dear and faithful Brother to me, and to my Children, in all our Tryals and Sufferings. . . . he would not have failed to come to see us night or day over two dangerous Sands, if it had been in the deep of Winter, many a time hath he done so of his own accord; and for the most part I have been sensible of his coming before he came, so near and dear was he unto me.[11]

Carry on walking, and on your right, just behind a farm called Greenbank, is a small paddock, with new trees and grazing sheep. This was reputedly an early Friends' burial ground.

Drive on to Nether Kellet and turn left to Halton (SD 502650). Fox preached at "Halton steeple-house by the water-side"[11] one Sunday, and a meeting was "settled" here later. The large church, St Wilfrid's, overlooks the Lune, and, except for the tower, has been rebuilt since Fox's day.

If you head for Slyne you can take the A6 to Kendal.

Other places of interest
Levens Hall and Gardens (SD 495851). Based on a 13th-century pele tower, the hall is Elizabethan, with Jacobean furniture, and has famous topiary gardens.
Sizergh Castle and Garden (SD 498879). A National Trust property, this is a fine 12th–13th-century manor house, furnished in Tudor and Stuart style.
Low Sizergh Barn (SD 502877) has a shop with fresh produce from the farm, a tearoom and a craft shop.
Kirkby Lonsdale is a beautiful town on the River Lune, crossed by 'Devil's Bridge'. Above it stands the magnificent St. Mary's Church, of Norman foundation, which contains significant Norman and 12th- and 13th-century features. Next to it a short public footpath leads to the famous 'Ruskin's View' over the river, which Ruskin

praised and J.M.W. Turner painted. Brontë enthusiasts may recognise Kirkby Lonsdale as 'Lowton' in *Jane Eyre*. The Clergy Daughters' School at nearby Cowan Bridge (not open to the public; 3 miles, 4.8 km along on the A65 toward Settle), where Charlotte and Emily Brontë and two of their sisters went to school, was 'Lowood' in the same novel.

7

Kendal

*Kendal – Underbarrow – Newton, Staveley and Lindale –
Cartmel – Holker – Bouth and Colton*

George Fox's route was Kendal, Underbarrow, Crosthwaite, High Newton, Staveley, Lindale, Cartmel, Bouth, Colton, Swarthmoor.

Kendal

Kendal (SD 518928) is 6 miles (9.6 km) from Preston Patrick. A flourishing market town of grey limestone, it was for centuries known as a centre for weaving and trading in woollen cloth throughout England.

Fox preached in the old Moot Hall, since replaced. The double-aisled parish church, down on the river bank, dates mainly from the thirteenth to the fifteenth century. There in 1650 Thomas Taylor (see under Preston Patrick, p. 38) won a heated debate with three ministers on the subject of infant baptism. Several early Friends were from Kendal, including Elizabeth Fletcher, who was cruelly treated by Oxford students in 1654, when she was 16, and died early after pioneer work in Ireland. Elizabeth Leavens shared her fate for preaching in Oxford and was later married to Thomas Holme, also of Kendal: the couple went to South Wales as Quaker missionaries. Ann Audland of Preston Patrick was originally from here.

Kendal gave its name to the Kendal Fund, which Margaret Fell and other Quaker women established to provide for the needs of travelling missionaries, poor Friends and schoolmasters: among other educational assets it provided Greek and Hebrew dictionaries for Thomas Lawson's school (see next chapter).

The Friends' school in Stramongate was founded in 1698 and closed in 1932. John Dalton (1766–1844), 'father of modern chemistry', taught there. Sir Arthur Stanley Eddington, Quaker astrophysicist, was born at the school in 1882, when his father was headmaster.

Kendal meeting house was built originally in 1688, and superseded by a large, stately new building on the same site in 1816. In 1994 the meeting house became the home of the Quaker Tapestry Exhibition, now known throughout the country and probably the world. Anne Wynn-Wilson of Taunton began the project in 1981, inspired by the Bayeux Tapestry. Nearly 4,000 people from 15 countries, including children, participated in the work, which took 15 years to complete. Embroidered on seventy-seven 21-by-25 inch panels of specially woven wool cloth, it recounts the history of

Quakerism from the beginning to the present. For example, we see George Fox preaching on Firbank Fell; the historic trial of William Penn and William Meade, which established the freedom of juries from coercion; the Peterloo Massacre with Manchester meeting house used as a refuge; and a parade of famous scientists – Dr John Fothergill, Joseph Lister and Thomas Hodgkin in medicine, John Dalton, Arthur Eddington, and crystallographer Kathleen Lonsdale; and Quaker railway pioneers such as George Bradshaw, who published the timetables. There is a garden outside which includes plants connected with Quaker botanists, who appear on one panel.

Anne Wynn-Wilson, who seems to have been divinely inspired as any early Friend, described the tapestry as an "experiment in education, communication and community experience". But "It could also be seen", says Jennie Levin in her descriptive book on the project, "as a celebration of the imagination, craftsmanship, tenacity and determination of the Quakers of the late twentieth century who made it".[1]

This stunning exhibition is open March to October: between seasons it tours.[2] Embroidery courses are available at the centre – in keeping with the Quaker Tapestry project, and to encourage wider use of the skills and techniques. This echoes Ruskin's attempts to encourage crafts in the area: he gave lectures in this building.

Fellside Burial Ground, Kendal: go up Allhallows Lane, turn left on Low Fellside and left again up a cobbled walkway, Sepulchre Lane. A sign on the left-hand side just past its gate explains that this was a Quaker burial ground bought in 1656, given to the town in the 19th century. Now it's a tiny, extremely peaceful grassy park with benches on the fell-side.

Other places of interest in Kendal
Kendal Castle, 13th century, is on the opposite river bank; the birthplace of Catherine Parr, it is now an attractive ruin with good countryside views.
Abbot Hall and the Museum of Lakeland Life: the former has a fine collection of British artists. In the latter are examples of woodwork by Quaker craftsmen Arthur Simpson, a member of the Arts and Crafts movement, and Stanley Davies. There are also

exhibitions on Arthur Ransome, the wool trade and period room furnishing. The first director, Helen Kapp, who established the collection, belonged to Brigflatts Meeting.

Arts and Crafts houses can be seen all round the town. Particularly have a look at Gillingate and Allhallows Lane. Littleholme, 103 Sedbergh Road, was designed by C.F.A. Voysey for his friend Arthur Simpson.

Underbarrow

After Kendal, George Fox's next stop was Underbarrow (SD 465915), about 1 mile (1.6 km) over the hill to the west of Kendal, reached via the stony ridge, Scout Scar. Follow the road marked Underbarrow at the northern entrance to Kendal. It is worth a stop in the car park en route to walk below Scout Scar, which is forested and features interesting vegetation. Fox walked, accompanied by others, and talked along the way with 17-year-old Edward Burrough, who was from Underbarrow. Soon after, when Edward told his parents he had become a Friend, they threw him out. He quickly became one of the movement's leaders, working with Francis Howgill to establish Quakerism in London, travelling to Ireland twice and on one occasion appealing to Charles II on behalf of imprisoned Friends. It was he who, along with James Nayler, convinced Thomas Ellwood, John Milton's secretary. Burrough died at 27 of prison fever in Newgate, a few days after Richard Hubberthorne, the king's order for his release having been purposely delayed.

Fox stayed the night with Miles Bateman at Tullithwaite Hall (SD 472909), south of the road from Kendal to Crosthwaite; it was rebuilt in the early 19th century smaller than the old building, of which very little survives. A sign on the way to it points to Ulverston, reminding us this was where Fox was headed.

The local priest came to dinner at Bateman's and there was discussion of whether to hold a meeting so Fox could speak at Underbarrow Chapel (the chapel has been pulled down, though its bell hangs in the modern building). As he walked next morning "on top of the bank", some poor travellers appeared. His companions gave them nothing, calling them cheats, but Fox ran after them, while the others breakfasted, and gave them money. Though the intended meeting was placed further in doubt by superstitious fear that Fox could not have gone so far so quickly had he not been bewitched, it went ahead, and many were convinced. A meeting was settled there, first called Underbarrow, later Crook Meeting; the building was demolished in 1844 but the burial ground remains (SD 438951).

Fox went on to John Dickinson's house in Crosthwaite, no longer standing.

Newton, Staveley and Lindale

David Boulton attempted to find Fox's route over the fells after Underbarrow and Newton-in-Cartmel, but the steepness of the terrain makes this very difficult. It would be best to take the A5074 after Underbarrow, and then the A590 acts as a corridor connecting these places, though you will find them in the unchronological order Lindale–Newton–Staveley, and then need to go back again. George Fox came from Underbarrow to James Taylor's at Newton-in-Cartmel (High Newton, bypassed by the A590).

About 1 mile (1.6 km) north of High Newton is the meeting house of 1677 at Height, or Cartmel Height, now a private house (SD 407848). This is an isolated spot: if you drive there, go back the way you came, since the roads further on are very high and narrow.

On Sunday 20 June Fox came to Staveley-in-Cartmel (SD 379862), not to be confused with the larger Staveley near Kendal. It is on a road which loops through it before the junction of the A590 and the A592 (which runs parallel to Lake Windermere). A small attractive village, its church was built twenty-six years later than the one at which Fox tried to preach, where the "rude" people, led by their minister Gabriel Camelford, tossed him over the graveyard wall.[3] He preached at an alehouse instead. It is not clear where the graveyard was then, but if the wall was in the direction of the current church hall, it would have been a nasty fall.

That afternoon, Fox went on to Lindale (SD 415805). As you take the A590 back toward Kendal, this is a turn to the right. As you enter it down a hill, you glimpse sea and sands. Fox preached at the chapel there – since replaced – then walked westward to the north of Morecambe Bay.

Cartmel

The Priory Church in Cartmel (SD 382787) is almost the only remnant of the 12th-century Augustinian Priory, apart from the gatehouse. It has a double tower of a style unique in England, with the upper portion set at a 45 degree angle to the lower. Saved from destruction by the claim that it was a parish church, it rises huge and beautiful, its ceiling reaching for the sky, full of light because the stained glass over the altar is confined to a small area of a big, otherwise clear window. The differently tinted panes of clearer glass make it look as if the tree outside the window is in bloom. The choir stalls are sublimely carved, with bunches of grapes and intricate tracery. The 17th-century choir screens are similar in workmanship to a fireplace in Swarthmoor Hall. The guidebook notes that George Fox visited Cartmel in 1652, and, when the vicar refused to dispute with him, spoke to parishioners. "Fox," it goes on, "was a redoubtable arguer and the Vicar probably felt that he would not be able to hold his own".[4]

Cartmel meeting house (SD 383786), dating from the mid-19th century, is a little way up Haggs Lane, the road toward Grange, on the right.

Holker

For nearby Holker, see Chapter 9.

Bouth and Colton

Fox went on northwest through Bouth (SD 329857), where he met Captain Adam Sandys, Chief Constable of Ulverston, whom he tried to convince. Fox remarks that if Sandys "could have had the world and Truth together, he would have received it", but was "a chaffy, light man".[5] Though Sandys did not become a Friend, some of his relations did, including his daughter Hester, who married Thomas Rawlinson, manager of Force Forge for the Fells.

Bouth today is a very small village with farmland on all sides. Colton (SD 316860) is up a hill. Going this way, after Colton you lose the back roads to Ulverston and have to go onto the A590, so it may be sensible to go by the A590 from the start.

8

Swarthmoor

Swarthmoor Hall – Swarthmoor Meeting House – Furness Abbey – Ulverston – Aldingham – Rampside – Sunbrick – Walney Island

Swarthmoor Hall

George Fox approached Swarthmoor Hall via Dalton-in-Furness and Walney Island, but we will begin with the Hall and cover the rest of his journey through Furness afterwards.

On the A590, at the second roundabout in Ulverston (SD 288783), take the turning toward Scales–Lightburn Trading Estate–Station. Here also is a brown sign, low down, saying "Swarthmoor Hall 1 mile" (1.6 km). After you pass the station on the right, another brown sign on the left points to Swarthmoor Hall (SD 282773) ½ mile (0.8 km) up Urswick Road, then another on the same side says ¼ mile (0.4 km) down Swarthmoor Hall Lane. Turn right into the car park. You may park there *only* while visiting the Hall. The Hall has conference facilities and accommodation and runs courses of various sorts throughout the year. Meeting for worship is held every Thursday, 12.30–1.00.

Attorney George Fell of Hawkswell probably built Swarthmoor Hall around 1586. The name, spelled variously (then as now) 'Swarthmoor' and 'Swarthmore', means 'black moor'. A plain, L-shaped three-storey building, ¾ mile (1.2 km) from the market town of Ulverston, the house was much larger originally. Thomas and Margaret Fell's grandson John Abraham had to sell it in 1731, after which it was inhabited by a series of tenant farmers and portions collapsed or were torn down. It was acquired in 1912 by Emma Clarke Abraham, a direct descendant of the Fells, who renovated it and added her own artwork in the carving and panelling for the Great Hall and study. The Society of Friends bought it in 1954.

Thomas Fell, who had by 1632 inherited the Hall from his attorney father George, was one of the most powerful men of the region. A Puritan in a loyalist area, he had been a member of the Long Parliament. He married Margaret Askew, daughter of a neighbouring landowner, sixteen years his junior. They had seven daughters and one son. The Fells attended St Mary's Church in Ulverston, where Judge Fell had probably been responsible for the appointment of the minister, Independent William Lampitt. Margaret Fell, though she attended this church, had been a Seeker for twenty years. Swarthmoor Hall was known for its hospitality to travelling ministers, and George Fox would have been attracted by the possibility of convincing Thomas Fell, who had influence with Cromwell. Both the Fells were absent, but he found minister Lampitt there and disputed with him.

That night when Margaret Fell returned, the children told her, somewhat to her discomfiture, that Fox had disagreed with her minister. "So," says Fox, "at night we had a great deal of reasoning and I declared the Truth to her and her family."[1] A day or two later Fox accompanied her to church and preached after the congregational singing had ended. Judge Sawrey attempted to lead him out, but Margaret Fell stood by him. On his return to Swarthmoor, Margaret Fell and members of her family and household were convinced. Several members of the household, including servants, later served as Quaker missionaries.

Fox went back toward Kendal, and was returning to the Sedbergh area when a message arrived from Margaret Fell that her husband had returned. Setting out again for Swarthmoor Hall, he found rumours had spread in the Ulverston area that he had bewitched the Fell family. This was a serious accusation: witchcraft was believed to be a real danger, and was a capital offence. After dinner, Fox answered the accusations and false reports to Fell's satisfaction. Two days later, the first meeting for worship was held at Swarthmoor with Judge Fell's permission.

From this point on, meetings continued regularly at Swarthmoor Hall. It is traditionally thought that they took place in the room described as the Great Hall, and Judge Fell is said to have sat next door in the room now called his study with the door open, hearing but not participating. He could not, if he had wanted to, have become a Friend and maintained his position – a position vitally important to the protection of Friends. Swarthmoor Hall became the centre for communication among Quakers. It was here that they came to recuperate after imprisonment and the tribulations and abuse that attended itinerant preaching. Here they wrote many of their pamphlets. Margaret Fell also used the Hall to administer the Kendal Fund and to keep in constant touch with Friends in all parts of the country.

There is an audio guide to accompany you round the house. The bible in 'Fell's study', published in 1541, a gift of George Fox to the meeting, is one of the oldest complete bibles in English. The study also contains the chair in which, reputedly, John Woolman died in York. One of the most unusual features of the house is the staircase, "built around four continuous square newels", forming a well 2 ft (65 cm) square, with turned balusters.[2] This is one of three or four examples of a four-post newel in England. Originally a roof support, it now ends about 4 feet (1.3 m) from the roof, showing that the roof pitch has been changed.

Most of the furnishings are not from here, but were collected recently and are appropriate to the period and status of the Fells, but the bed in the room identified as the Fells' is said to be original. Emma Clarke Abraham cut off the bottom two posts and incorporated them in the study fireplace. Carving round the bedroom fireplace, from the first half of the 18th century, is the same pattern as the choir screens in Cartmel Priory Church, probably by the same craftsman.

'George Fox's Room' contains a four-poster 'travelling bed', which is extremely heavy, so probably didn't do much travelling. It was given to Fox in Barbados and left by him for Friends' use, along with his sea chest, with bottles in it, and the chair given him by Robert Widders of Over Kellet, "to stand in the house . . . so that Friends . . . may have a bed to lie on, and a chair to sit in, and a bottle to hold a little water to drink".[3] Another chest, with his initials and "1675" on top, is thought to have come with him out of Worcester gaol.

The top floor, where it is claimed sixty of Cromwell's troops were once billeted, is an exhibition room. Among the artefacts displayed are a bed which belonged to Robert Widders of Over Kellet (see Chapter 6) and a 1549 'treacle Bible', so called because it contained the words, "Is there no tryacle in Gilead?". (The word 'treacle' signified originally a medicinal salve.) **Warning: do watch your head when going in and particularly out of this door!**

To the right of and behind the house, walk through what used to be an avenue of yews, allegedly planted by Judge Fell on the birth of each of his children, to the wildflower meadow, spectacular with crocuses in early spring. All the Fells' daughters became Friends and all married Friends; the only son, George, became a source of anxiety. William Caton, for a while his tutor, and Margaret Fell's secretary, was one of the 'Valiant Sixty'; he died in Holland at the age of 29.

Other members of the Swarthmoor household who became Friends and travelled to spread the Quaker message were Thomas Salthouse, the steward; Leonard Fell, a retainer whose relationship, if any, to the judge's family is unknown, as is his exact position in the household; Henry Fell, the judge's clerk; and Ann Clayton, a maid-servant. Thomas Salthouse, one of four brothers all of whom became Friends, was an accomplished preacher, and travelled extensively in the south-west. Leonard Fell travelled widely through England and Scotland and suffered many imprisonments; Henry Fell, a man of considerable education, went to the West Indies, the continent of Europe and the Near East, as well as many parts of England; Ann Clayton went to the West Indies and to Rhode Island, where she married the Quaker Governor and, after his death, his successor.

After Judge Fell's death in 1658 Swarthmoor Friends were persecuted relentlessly by neighbouring justices, and Margaret Fell herself suffered trials and imprisonments. In 1669 she married George Fox, though the circumstances of their lives demanded long periods of separation. George Fox was able to spend only two further periods at Swarthmoor Hall: one of twenty-one months in 1675–6, and one of twenty months in 1678–80. In his later years he made his headquarters near London in the homes of his step-daughters Margaret Rous and Sarah Meade, and Margaret would travel south from Swarthmoor to visit him.

The walk from the Hall to Ulverston (park elsewhere first) is tranquil and worthwhile. It is found by going down the drive to the left as you face the Hall. If you want to walk to Swarthmoor from Ulverston, pass the station, then The Drive on the right, and before St. Mary's School is a metal gate with a sign saying "Public Footpath Swarthmoor Hall ½ mile" (0.6 km).

Swarthmoor Meeting House

The Friends' burial ground was purchased in 1669. In 1687 George Fox, anticipating that the Society would outgrow the Hall as a meeting place, bought the land for a meeting house, which was built the next year. Arrangements should be made with the manager at the Hall to visit the meeting house outside Sunday worship time. It is found by walking to the left on leaving Swarthmoor Hall, crossing Urswick Road, and going part way down Meeting House Lane. It is on the left, behind a locked gate. Over the entrance is inscribed "EX DONO: GF, 1688". Fox directed that the way to it should be paved, "that Friends may go dry to Meeting".[4] The benches and panelling (added in the early 19th century) are painted grey. Benches are at the back, chairs in a circle in the middle. This interesting building has a sloping balcony, with backless benches, where women's meetings were held. Panels open out into the main meeting area. On the ground floor is a separate room, originally used as a schoolroom. A kitchen and large social room have been made from the former stables.

Furness and the Abbey
George Fox came into the area via Dalton-in-Furness, a mining centre in the 17th century. The church where "The people grew brutish and fell of ringing the bells" when Fox preached there[5] was replaced in the 19th century; there is no longer much of interest in Dalton except a pele tower, not open. Marsh Grange (SD 221798), Margaret Fell's original home, is nearby, 1½ miles (2.4 km) from Ireleth. Now surrounded by a high wall, it cannot be seen. Since Margaret Fell's time it has been partly destroyed by fire. Pictures of it before and after the fire can be seen in Swarthmoor Hall.

Furness needed to be self-sufficient, cut off from the south of the country by Morecambe Bay, whose tentacles intersect it at various points, necessitating either crossing – which can be dangerous – or going round. It is also cut off to the north by the Furness Fells. The area had been ruled up to the Reformation by the Cistercian Furness Abbey (SD 220715) founded in 1127, the abbot having all the powers of mediaeval lordship. Estates were organised into blocks of land called granges, with mixed farming: corn, sheep and cattle. The area was vulnerable to Scots invasions, the reason for the Abbot's Castle on Piel Island (see page 61). After the Reformation, the abbey, land and administration of the region were annexed by the royal Duchy of Lancaster. The ruins of the abbey, mostly mid-12th century, very impressive red sandstone, are administered by English Heritage.

Ulverston

Ulverston was the centre of trade in the area, and the market, on the western side of the town, dealt in corn, oats and woven goods: it was later overtaken in size by Barrow. Stan Laurel was born Arthur Stanley Jefferson in Ulverston: the Laurel and Hardy Museum, at the former Roxy cinema, has biographical material, memorabilia and films showing constantly.

St Mary's Church (SD 288786) is not easy to find. If you get a map of the town, you can find it much more easily on foot than by car. Its steeple can't be spotted from afar, because it has only a "stubby crenellated tower".[6] It is on Church Walk, which is lined with comfortable Victorian houses. Some parts are Norman, some 16th century, the rest Victorian.

This is the church referred to by George Fox as the 'steeple-house', where William Lampitt ministered and where Judge Fell lies buried in an unmarked grave. George Fox spoke there on Thursday 1 July 1652, a day or two after his arrival at Swarthmoor Hall, and his words so touched the heart of Margaret Fell that she wept in her pew. On a later visit the same year, he preached in the church again on a 'lecture day', when anyone might speak with permission, but on this occasion he was mobbed with the assent of Judge Sawrey of Plumpton Hall, then consigned to officers to be whipped and put out of town.[7] Plumpton Hall is to the east of Ulverston, not far from the railway viaduct crossing the Leven channel.

In Ulverston take the A5087 to Bardsea and Coast Road toward Barrow.

Aldingham

After coming to Swarthmoor Hall, George Fox preached at Aldingham church (SD 283710): "The priest told me Matthew, Mark, Luke and John were the Gospel, I told him the Gospel was the power of God".[8] On another occasion, women Friends verbally attacked the Aldingham priest. There is nothing in this quiet village now except a stately nursing home, five houses and the parish church of St Cuthbert, which is open and welcoming. Full of interesting original features and in a restful location beside the sea, it is thought to date from the mid-12th century. Its graveyard is just above a sandy beach. Prayer must surely have been valid here too. The leaflet suggests you rest for a moment and "Let the peace of this place and its seaside location surround you".

Rampside
Rampside (SD 235661) is significant for its association with Thomas Lawson, schoolmaster and botanist. The 21-year-old Lawson, having been a year at Cambridge, was acting as minister in St Michael's Church. When George Fox came on here after Aldingham, Lawson unhesitatingly offered him his pulpit and soon after became a Friend. One of the 'Valiant Sixty', he travelled to spread Quakerism in the south of England, and on the way observed the plants of the areas he visited. He opened an effective school at Great Strickland but was eventually arrested for not having a licence. After that he went to Swarthmoor Hall and turned his attention to natural history. The Reformation had emphasised botanic study: "God was to be studied in the perfection of plants",[9] and at the same time there was emerging a new attitude to science based on observation and experiment rather than tradition and authority. Both traditions stimulated Lawson, who was a pioneer in the study and cataloguing of plant distribution.

Rampside was a port in the mid-17th century. Now you can drive onto a narrow causeway surrounded by the sea, from which you can see Piel Island and Piel Castle. This is the place commemorated by Wordsworth in his "Elegiac Stanzas, Suggested by a Picture of Peele Castle in a Storm, Painted by Sir George Beaumont". Wordsworth had stayed at Rampside in his youth, when the sea was tranquil. But the picture of the castle in a storm with a ship about to be wrecked later called to mind the death at sea of his brother John.

Go back to the A5087, turn left toward Barrow, and you'll see St Michael's Church on the left, a newer version in the same location as Thomas Lawson's, looking down over farmland to the sea.

Sunbrick
For Sunbrick or Sunbreck (SD 286739) burial ground, from Swarthmoor meeting house go right on Mountbarrow Road, and in about 2 miles (3.2 km) cross a cattle grid. After it, turn at the *second* left-hand turn (pass the one that goes to Bardsea in one direction,

Urswick in the other). This is a steep, narrow road. Carry on along it, looking very carefully to the right until, immediately before the farm on the right-hand side, there is a stone wall which has an opening with a huge Lakeland slate as lintel. There is no gate. Right inside is a sign saying:

> SOCIETY OF FRIENDS SUNBRICK BURIAL GROUND BETWEEN THE YEARS 1654-1767 THERE WERE BURIED 227 FRIENDS AMONG WHOM MARGARET FOX WIFE FIRST OF JUDGE THOMAS FELL AND SECONDLY OF GEORGE FOX FOUNDER OF THE SOCIETY OF FRIENDS

It is inspiring here to remember Margaret Fell as the first Friend to articulate the Peace Testimony in an assurance to Charles II and the Houses of Parliament in April 1660: "We are a People that follows after those things that make for Peace, Love, and Unity, and do deny and bear our Testimony against all Strife, and Wars, and Contentions. . . . Our weapons are *not Carnal*, but *Spiritual* . . ."[10]

There are no gravestones. The sea is visible over the wall in two directions. Gentle trees abide here, and sheep graze in obvious safety. In addition to seagulls, I heard the cry of peacocks from the farm next door.

If you drive farther down the road toward the sea, taking the left-hand fork at the T junction, looking to the left you will see a crescent area of very short grass, and a short cut grass path leading to a prehistoric stone circle (SD 292739).

Go back to the A590 and on to Barrow, a town which did not exist in Fox's day.

Walney Island

Follow signs in Barrow to Walney Island and cross the bridge to it (SD 188688), turning right immediately on reaching the island. (If you go in the other direction you will come to a stretch of windswept seaside grasses and wild flowers, a bird sanctuary.) Drive on until you reach the end of the line of boats on the beach. Directly opposite that a sign says "North Scale" on a wall beside the road, at a point where the speed limit becomes 20 mph. Behind the 20 mph sign, just beyond where the road to the left goes to Border Kennels, is the house which was home to James Lancaster (SD 183697), the first islander to become a Friend, a farmer in a predominantly fishing community. Rendered and updated, the house does not at first look old. In George Fox's time one could, at low tide, walk across to the island. At other times it was necessary to go by boat.

By the end of the summer, James Nayler had come to join Fox at Swarthmoor Hall. Together they went to Walney Island and were attacked by people sent by James Lancaster's wife. They had nearly been drowned, as well as being severely beaten, when Lancaster rowed Fox to the mainland, then came back for Nayler. Judge Fell sent warrants against the attackers. It is satisfying to learn that Mrs Lancaster later became a Friend.

9
Lancaster

Furness was part of Lancashire until the county of Cumbria was created in 1974, so there were administrative and legal reasons why people like the Fells needed to be connected with Lancaster as the county town, despite being separated by Morecambe Bay and its dangerous sands. They would have crossed in two stages, between Ulverston and Cark, and between Kents Bank (near Grange-over-Sands) and Hest Bank (north of Lancaster). If you wish to do this yourself, it is absolutely essential to be taken by one of the official guides (see *Planning your pilgrimage*).

Holker

On the route from Swarthmoor to Lancaster, Holker Hall (SD 359775) near Cark-in-Cartmel is a stately home with gardens, worth a visit for itself and for associations with George Fox. Thomas Preston, its 17th-century owner, who had leased the tithes of Cartmel parish, was one of the chief regional persecutors of Quakers. On one occasion in 1663, George Fox and Margaret Fell were taken from Swarthmoor to Holker Hall for examination, the prelude to George Fox's trial and long imprisonments in Lancaster and Scarborough. (For other places around Cartmel see Chapter 7.)

Lancaster

On his first visit to Lancaster, after he had come to Swarthmoor Hall, Fox preached at the market cross and settled a meeting. The next Sunday he preached to a crowd in the street, after which he went up the castle hill and "declared truth" to the priest and congregation at the Priory Church (SD 474619), next to the castle. He was stoned all the way to St. Leonardsgate, where he took refuge in the shop of John Lawson, who became a Friend. The church, founded as part of a Benedictine priory around 1094, was built on a site once used by the Romans. Remains of a Roman bath house can be seen nearby.

Quakers stood out in Lancaster, a place particularly observant of ceremony and folk customs, both of which they opposed. It was a violent town, whereas Quakers were (ultimately) pacifists. And it was a class-conscious place: Quaker refusal to be so was offensive.[1]

The castle (SD 473619) was both the courthouse and the county jail until 2011. Numerous Friends were imprisoned in Lancaster

Castle for sedition, for holding meetings and for refusing to take oaths. Friends believed, and still do, in a single standard of truth, according to the Bible: "I say to you swear not at all . . . let your communication be, Yea, yea; Nay, nay; for whatsoever is more than these cometh of evil".[2]

Tours focusing on Quaker history are available. A tour of the castle includes viewing instruments of torture and the chance to enter a cell. If someone shuts the door, darkness is total. But nothing can bring to our imagination the stench from many people crowded in a cell having to use a bucket or the straw on the floor to relieve themselves. The unsanitary conditions led to disease, and many Friends died in prison, thirteen in Lancaster Castle. Lancaster Friends ministered to the prisoners' needs, with fuel and candles supplied by Lancashire Quarterly Meeting.

George Fox was tried at Lancaster Castle three times and imprisoned there twice, for a total of two and a half years, for sedition and refusing to take the oath. He was incarcerated in a tower, which he called his "dark house", to the right of Shire Hall. On the first occasion when he was tried there, in 1652, he was acquitted and allowed to preach in open court. Then in 1660, at the Restoration, he was accused of plotting against the King and imprisoned some months, but released after Margaret Fell had pled for him in person to the King. In 1663 he was tried for sedition and refusal to take the Oath of Allegiance. He was imprisoned in Lancaster, then transferred to Scarborough Castle until 1666. These sufferings undermined his health.

Margaret Fell was imprisoned there three times, for a total of four years, in 1664, in 1670–1 and in 1683. On the first occasion she received the sentence of *praemunire*, which involved being cut off from the King's protection, surrender to the King of all her property and indefinite imprisonment. Her heroic reply to the judge was, "Although I am out of the King's Protection, yet I am not out of the Protection of the Almighty God".[3]

Lancaster meeting house (SD 472616), on Meeting House Lane near the castle, was built in 1677, rebuilt in 1708 because it was too small, then extended further in 1779 and 1789. It is a well-attended meeting today.

10

The Lake District

*Rookhow and Force Forge – Windermere – Rydal – Grasmere
– Hawkshead and Colthouse – Near Sawrey – Brantwood –
Cockermouth – Pardshaw – Mosedale*

CHAPTER 10 – THE LAKE DISTRICT

Though Fox did not spend much time in the Lake District, many visitors to '1652 Country' will wish to include it in a trip, being so near. To many, like myself, it is the most beautiful place on earth: it is now a national park, and as well as its outstanding natural beauty it has unrivalled cultural associations. There are magnificent fell walks all through the Lake District, as well as the lakes themselves, each different. Apart from the natural surroundings, there are innumerable other attractions, from which I have selected a very few, in addition to the interesting early Friends' meeting houses.

The area is known particularly in association with the Romantic movement in literature. Several Romantic attitudes seem to have been heralded by Quakerism: regard for the individual, social concern, the sense of innocence, belief in essential human goodness. William Wordsworth, his sister Dorothy and Samuel Taylor Coleridge had several Quaker friends. Wordsworth wrote a poem to one of them, Thomas Wilkinson: "To the Spade of a Friend".

One of the things that makes the Lake District so exciting is that the weather is very changeable and may differ radically from place to place within a smallish geographical compass. It is possible to be in calm weather and warm sunshine near Lake Windermere and cross over the Kirkstone Pass to find Ullswater in heavy cloud and rain, or to be on a mountaintop unable to move for heavy rain, looking down at a valley bathed in sunshine.

Rookhow and Force Forge

Rookhow Meeting House (SD 332896) is in Grizedale Forest between Ulverston and Hawkshead, near Bouth (see Chapter 7). Only 9 miles (14.4 km) from Ulverston, it is 10 minutes on winding valley roads from the A590 at Newby Bridge, but until you know the way you are advised to follow the A590 from Ulverston to Greenodd, then the A5092 (sign Whitehaven / Workington) for just over ½ mile (1 km); then the *first right* (sign Colton / Oxen Park) for about 5 miles (8 km). Rookhow is on the left, immediately after you see (but do not follow!) the sign for Ickenthwaite.

If you come via Hawkshead, take the road to Grizedale, go through it, then Satterthwaite. You will pass Force Mill village on your right; then on the left is Force Forge village. There is no indication of where the actual forge stood. It has been suggested it was at Force Mill,[1] likely because the river runs through it. The forge was owned and run by Margaret Fell and her daughters from 1658 to 1681. There was an acrimonious conflict between Margaret Fell and the forge manager Thomas Rawlinson, a Quaker, son of Captain William Rawlinson of Graythwaite and Rusland Hall. Rawlinson ultimately bought the forge from the Fells.[2]

If you carry on along this road, you'll eventually see a steep uphill drive, in crescent shape, which goes to Rookhow (labelled only on the other side). This meeting house (SD 332896) was built in 1725 as a place specifically to hold monthly business meetings for the Swarthmoor area. Meeting for worship occurs on the first Wednesday of every month. There is also a hostel in a former barn, with about 20 beds in two rooms and a kitchen/dining room.

Behind the meeting house is what used to be called Abbot's Oak Wood (because it was originally owned by Furness Abbey), now Quaker Wood. It now contains a yurt and a wigwam and paths for walking. Behind it is a hillside that has been untouched for centuries, trees left to rot where they fell.

Windermere

The first publishers of truth says that when some people in Windermere "came to be convinced later",[3] a meeting was settled there and a meeting house built. David Butler identifies this as the one at Mislet, closed 1822 and now in private occupation;[4] it is about 1 ½ miles (2.4 km) east from Windermere station, up the third turning to the left on the road to Staveley (SD 432996). The Quaker presence in Windermere now is Gatesbield, a retirement community which is also a local meeting, with worship each Sunday.

South of Windermere town, Blackwell is a magnificent Arts and Crafts house (SD 401946) with a room full of windows overlooking Lake Windermere. Its 'great hall', with 'minstrel's gallery' is downstairs, and upstairs are art exhibitions. It is furnished with fine examples of Arts and Crafts furniture and design, including that of Arthur Simpson. Its lunch room is excellent.

North of the town, near Troutbeck Bridge, Townend (NY 407024) was a yeoman farmer's house dating probably from 1626, its barn from 1666. Thus it represents a residence of the class from which early Friends were particularly drawn. It is run by the National Trust, open March–October.

Rydal

Rydal Mount (NY 362065), Wordsworth's later home, with the gardens he designed, is well worth seeing. The Coffin Route from just above Rydal Mount to Grasmere, on which coffins used to be carried for burial, is a good walk with superb views.

Grasmere

This is the location of the Quaker guest house, Glenthorne (NY 336076), which lies up Easedale Road on the left. This is a good walking centre, with excellent meals and home-baked cakes. Even if you don't stay at Glenthorne, there is a beautiful walk to Easedale Tarn and a waterfall near it, further up Easedale Road.

At Town End are Dove Cottage (NY 345071), Wordsworth's first adult home in the Lake District, and the Wordsworth Museum (www.wordsworth.org.uk; tel. 01539 435544). The museum has a permanent exhibition on the Romantic poets, and changing exhibits. The Wordsworth family graves are in St Oswald's churchyard. The church is interesting, built in the 11th and 15th centuries with two aisles, and two roofs joined to create a fascinating roof beam formation.

Hawkshead and Colthouse

In Hawkshead (SD 352982), Quakerism originated from a 'miracle' by George Fox, when he healed a boy who couldn't walk. The *Journal* describes a visit he paid in 1653, with Margaret Fell the younger and William Caton, when he found a crippled child in a Friend's house and was able to reach the source of his trouble: his family returned home after Fox had gone, and found the boy playing in the streets. "And so the Lord have the praise", concludes Fox.[5]

While attending the grammar school on the main road, Wordsworth lodged at the cottage of Ann Tyson, now a bed and breakfast, on Vicarage Lane.

Colthouse (SD 359984) is reachable from two directions. The

easier route is through Hawkshead: turn left toward Sawrey, then left again toward Wray. The meeting house is off a lane to the right. The narrower, steeper and slightly prettier route goes down the opposite side of Esthwaite Lake, through Low and High Wray. Take the B5682 from Clappersgate toward Hawkshead, then the left-hand turn signposted for Wray Castle and Low Wray Campsite, where there is also a National Trust sign. Go past these and through High Wray until you come to a sign on the left saying "150 metres to Quaker meeting house". Turn in, and it is on the right.

Further along the road on the left is the burial ground, previously an orchard, acquired in 1658. It is enclosed within stone walls, built into which are stone seats, so it could be used for worship. As persecution slackened and it became safe to meet indoors, the meeting house was built in 1688 and known initially as Hawkshead Meeting. It was registered in 1689, the year of the Toleration Act, which permitted religious gatherings to occur in buildings other than churches.

Very near is the later home of the Tysons, with whom Wordsworth continued to live while in school at Hawkshead. It is alleged he sometimes attended Colthouse Meeting while there.[6] Beatrix Potter certainly did in 1896, according to her journal, and "liked it very much".[7] There were 20–30 attenders when she was there, fewer now.

Near Sawrey

Continuing from Hawkshead or from Colthouse Meeting, you will come to Beatrix Potter's house and garden on your right (SD 368957). Inside are furniture and items she owned, and displays of her illustrations.

Brantwood

On the banks of Coniston Water, Brantwood was the home of John Ruskin in later life (SD 312958), adapted to his design. The gardens have recently been restored. The house contains artwork of Ruskin and his period and is furnished similarly to the way it was when he lived there. This lake inspired Arthur Ransome's *Swallows and Amazons*.

Cockermouth

George Fox, John Audland and Edward Burrough reached the Cockermouth area in 1653. George Fox preached at Cockermouth: "and when the priest had done I began to speak and the people to be rude, but the soldiers told them we had broken no law and then they were quiet." (Fox p. 153). There is a Quaker meeting house (NY 124305) originally of 1688 but rebuilt 1782 and 1884.

Wordsworth's childhood home (NY 122309) is owned by the National Trust. Its garden borders the River Cocker.

Pardshaw

To get to Pardshaw meeting house (NX 104256) take the A66 around Cockermouth, and at the roundabout at the Wellington Sheep and Wool Centre, take the B5086 for 3 miles (4.8 km), passing Eaglesfield (NX 095284). You may want to turn off the main road here and visit Eaglesfield to see the Friends burial ground to the west of the village and the small cottage where John Dalton was born, which has a plaque identifying it. Turn left, where the sign says "Pardshaw Hall", and then right at the end of this road, deeply rutted when I was last there. Park in front of the carriage shed, which looks rather derelict, its windows boarded up. Behind the gate opposite, inside locked walls, you will find a schoolhouse, meeting house and stables, surrounding a burial ground. The smaller meeting room, probably originally for the women's meeting, is now used for meeting for worship, about half an hour at 7.00pm on the third Sunday of each month. It is still used for weddings and funerals.

The first publishers of truth says that after meeting had for a time been at Mosser Chapel, "Friends settled a meeting at . . . Peter Head's house, which was the first meeting that was settled in Cumberland, & many were convinced of the truth, that the houses could not contain them. But they met without doors, for many years, on a place called Pardshow Cragg, & abundance of Peple crowded to the Meets".[8] George Whitehead recalls meetings on Pardshaw Crag (which he calls "Pargee"): it was very cold in snow and sleet, but there were areas "where Sheep may shelter from the Windy and Stormy Side, so Friends commonly took the same Advantage to meet on the calmest Side". He goes on to reminisce about meetings in mountainous areas: "I remember when it has rained most of the Time at some Meetings where we have been very much wetted; and yet I do not remember that ever I got any Hurt thereby . . . ".[9] Friends nowadays are less hardy.

In 1672 a meeting house was built. In 1728 it was demolished and rebuilt with the same materials a short distance away.[10] A separate schoolhouse, which was attended by John Dalton, came next, and finally the coach house in 1879, for the widely scattered membership. Use declined in the 20th century, and the meeting house was closed in 1923. Later, the coach house was a hostel, where in the late 1960s I spent a week and tried to read Shakespeare aloud with three friends by gaslight. Electricity was added, but more recently vandalism forced the building's closure. Hostelling moved to the larger room in the meeting house, and the stables gained basins and a shower. If you look behind the shower you will see a manger. With fewer young Friends, this hostel ceased operating as well.

To get to Pardshaw Crag take the path behind the phone box next to the carriage shed. Go to the right, up to the fenced-in sheep pasture, then climb upward a little further.

Mosedale

In 1652 Fox, Burrough and Blaykling had a meeting in the barony of Graystoke, and "soon after a meeting was settled and yet remains, called Mosedale Meeting".[11] And it remains still. Turn off the A66 going toward Penrith at Mungrisdale. Go through Mungrisdale and follow signs for Mosedale (NY 356322), a very small hamlet which shelters under Carrock Fell, with Bowfell on one side. The area is barren of trees except in the Quaker graveyard. Turn into the car park to the right, available for walkers for a contribution, next to the graveyard. There are no gravestones, just a walled grass rectangle with benches, trees and wild flowers. The meeting house is on the road opposite. Meeting occurs every Sunday from April to October, and on the second and fourth Sundays from November to March. The meeting house is small and could be mistaken for a low barn. Based on an older building, it was constructed in 1702, with benches in a square and a minister's gallery at one end. Outside is a grassy area, open to public use.

11
Conclusion

Over the years from 1652 until today, the Society of Friends has undergone many changes. From the end of the 17th century, Friends reacted against years of persecution in a period of 'quietism', detached from the world outside. Being a 'peculiar people' originally meant being 'special' or 'distinctive', like the Jews in the Bible; the Peculiar Baptists took their name from this. But Quaker 'peculiarity' became associated with forms like standardised 'plain dress' – though Margaret Fell in 1698 had opposed the trend toward drabness, pointing to "changeable colours as the hills are";[1] 'plain language' ("thee" and "thy") continued, at least among family and close friends, well into the 20th century, and plain dress was still worn in a few isolated pockets of the United States at least as late as the 1960s.

Early Friends were extremely puritanical, avoiding theatre and other arts, a resistance which was still expressing itself in a sort of artistic clumsiness until well past the middle of the 20th century. Love of beauty is now part of the Society's active witness, and Friends number prominent artists of all sorts among members.

Quakerism has always defined itself in terms of continuing revelation. This comprehends and excuses – if it needs excusing – changes between 1652 and now. While mid-17th-century Quakers were openly enthusiastic about religion, sometimes doing strange things to show their enthusiasm, today's Friends are more reserved, and also more inclusive, ranging from devoted Christians to universalists and humanists. From the original insistence on being completely separate from – indeed hostile to – other religious organisations, many now support the 'churches together' movement. The focus is now less on spreading a message with missionary fervour than on trying to change the world for the better, combating poverty and injustice, supporting equality and promoting peaceful means of settling conflict.

What is the purpose of going on a 'pilgrimage'? For a denomination which has always believed that certain places and dates are no more significant than others, this is an important question. There is an aspect of history which is tangible, and going to places associated with historical occurrences might help us understand them, as landscape helps us understand the inspiration of artists. It certainly educates us in Quaker history with a vividness that no school course can succeed in doing. It may make us more conscious of the difference between Quakerism then and now, and lead us to consider what needs changing about the ways in which we presently conduct it. Many Friends are so busy doing good work that they spend little time in rest and reflection. Such a journey could serve that purpose. Is there something more? That depends on the 'pilgrim'. Perhaps a concept of 'sacred space' may help develop and maintain the sense of something above/ beyond reason. Some feel that holding a meeting for worship on Pendle Hill or Firbank Fell or at Swarthmoor Hall may deepen their experience in their own meetings.

A member of my own Friends' meeting, pondering my question on the relationship between Friends yesterday and today, suggests that early Friends in a time of religious and political turmoil were seekers after faith and a way of operating that made sense for their time. In today's turmoil, when we feel that things cannot go on as they are, Quakerism attracts people who are looking for something but are not yet clear what it is. They may find it in a Friends' meeting or want to join others there in seeking.

Friends' source of strength is still to wait silently, communing or hoping to commune with something beyond which is also part of themselves. In 1677 George Fox and Margaret Fell attended meeting in Brigflatts. Fox reported, according to the Ellwood edition of his *Journal*, "I had a Meeting at Brigflatts . . . and a very good Meeting it was . . . ".[2] As the Brigflatts warden remarked to me, "It's still going on".

12

Further reading

CHAPTER 12 – FURTHER READING

'Classic' accounts and more recent ones should be balanced against each other: William C. Braithwaite's two volumes, *The beginnings of Quakerism* and *The second period of Quakerism* are the standard history. More recently and at less length, John Punshon's *Portrait in Grey* gives an overall history of Quakerism. Barry Reay provides a corrective to the standard accounts in *The Quakers and the English revolution*, using non-Quaker sources to analyse how and why Quakers were feared as a threat. Christopher Hill's *The world turned upside down* gives a superb analysis of the various religious and political movements in the period when Quakerism began.

The standard biography of Margaret Fell was for a long time Isabel Ross, *Margaret Fell: the mother of Quakerism*. But Bonnelyn Young Kunze, from a feminist perspective, shows Margaret Fell as a rather autocratic and contentious Mother Superior in *Margaret Fell and the rise of Quakerism*. Though James Nayler is now much more appreciated than when the movement was in jeopardy through his trial for blasphemy, no totally satisfactory biography yet exists. The most recent, by David Neelon, is stylistically odd and unclear in organisation, discussions of Nayler's thoughts and writings abstruse and confusing. Leo Damrosch, *The sufferings of the Quaker Jesus*, seems competent and is readable. The best biography of George Fox is by H. Larry Ingle, *First among Friends*.

The most significant contemporary account of the founding days of Quakerism is the journal of George Fox, most accessible in the edition by John L. Nickalls. A Lancaster University project is working on a critical edition on the web of the journal in its various forms: www.lancs.ac.uk/fass/projects/quakers.

Immensely interesting is *The first publishers of truth*, edited by Norman Penney, with accounts by Friends of the early years of Quakerism in response to a questionnaire. It is available now as a reprint and (rather unreliably scanned) on the internet. Recent works focusing on the '1652 Country' are Donald A. Rooksby's *And sometime upon the hills*, which gives encyclopaedic listings of Quaker sites in the area, and David and Anthea Boulton's account of walking Fox's route, *In Fox's Footsteps*. An interesting discussion of the effect of pilgrimage to the area on Quakers today, by someone who has led many tours of the region, is Roy Stephenson's article '1652 Country: A land steeped in our faith' in *The Friend*,

8 October 2010. The pamphlet edited by Angus Winchester, *The 1652 Country: Planning your pilgrimage*, updated annually by the Society of Friends, is also available on the Britain Yearly Meeting website: www.quaker.org.uk.

Among studies of individuals, I found particularly interesting E. Jean Whittaker's biography of the botanist and educationist Thomas Lawson, *Thomas Lawson 1630–1691*, which contains a good account of travelling ministry in the early years of Quakerism. *The history of the life of Thomas Ellwood* (1714) is the superbly written autobiography of John Milton's secretary, including his conversion to Quakerism as a young man, and the difficulties it led to first within his family, later with the law. He was not from the north of England but the book shows Edward Burrough and James Nayler in action, and he was editor of Fox's *Journal*.

There are as many as 40 of the early founders of Quakerism included in the new *Oxford Dictionary of National Biography*. Joseph Besse's collection of Sufferings has been reprinted in regional volumes and indexed, showing the kind of persecution of early Friends that took place.

Friends' meeting houses and their history are detailed in David M. Butler's 2-volume *Quaker meeting houses*. It supersedes his earlier *Quaker meeting houses of the Lake Counties*, but that is more portable. A wonderful resource for buildings of the area, including meeting houses and Swarthmoor Hall, is Matthew Hyde's new version of Pevsner's *Buildings of England: Cumbria*.

To find out more about Quakers, contact the Quaker Life Outreach Section, Friends House, 173 Euston Road, London NW1 2BJ, freephone 0808 109 1651 or email outreach@quaker.org.uk.

13

Endnotes

Chapter 1
1. Daniel Defoe, *A tour through the whole island of Great Britain*, pp. 549–550.
2. J. D. Marshall, *Old Lakeland*, p. 56.
3. John Wilhelm Rowntree, *Essays and addresses*, p. 76.

Chapter 2
1. George Fox, *Journal*, ed. Nickalls, p. 58.
2. *Journal*, ed. Nickalls, p. 104.
3. Barry Reay, *The Quakers and the English revolution*, pp. 26–30.

Chapter 3
1. George Fox, *Journal*, ed. Nickalls, p. 104.

Chapter 4
1. David and Anthea Boulton, *In Fox's footsteps*, p. 26.
2. Norman Penny, ed., *First publishers of truth*, p. 242.
3. David Boulton, *Early Friends in Dent*, p. 19.
4. *First publishers of truth*, p. 329.
5. *Early Friends in Dent*, p. 24f.
6. *First publishers of truth*, p. 329.
7. *First publishers of truth*, p. 311.
8. George Fox, *Journal*, ed. Nickalls, p. 105.
9. *First publishers of truth*, p. 311.
10. *First publishers of truth*, p. 307.
11. *First publishers of truth*, p. 329.

Chapter 5
1. George Fox, *Journal*, ed. Nickalls, p. 106.
2. *Ibid*.
3. Hugh Barbour, *The Quakers in Puritan England*, p. 45.
4. George Whitehead, *The Christian progress of George Whitehead*, p. 5.
5. David and Anthea Boulton, *In Fox's footsteps*, p. 119.
6. *In Fox's footsteps*, p. 132.

7 See David Boulton, *Early Friends in Dent*, p. 40. He notes that the "Great Book" dates this as 1661, but the account in the Sedbergh manuscript is 1665, which as the contemporary local record seems more likely.
8 H. Larry Ingle, *First among Friends*, p. 263; *In Fox's footsteps*, p. 134.
9 Christopher Hill, *The world turned upside down*, p. 256.
10 Thomas Machell, *Antiquary on horseback*, p. 38.
11 *Journal*, ed. Nickalls, p. 108.
12 Norman Penny, ed., *First publishers of truth*, p. 251.
13 *Britannia*; 1610 edition (repr. 2003), vol. 2, p. 761.
14 *The world turned upside down*, p. 249.
15 *Quaker faith & practice*, 19.12.
16 David Neelon, *James Nayler: revolutionary to prophet*, p. 82.

Chapter 6
1 George Fox, *Journal*, ed. Nickalls, p. 110.
2 David and Anthea Boulton, *In Fox's footsteps*, p. 144.
3 John Woodman, *The journal and major essays*, pp. 185–186.
4 Norman Penny, ed., *First publishers of truth*, p. 254.
5 *First publishers of truth*, p. 244.
6 *First publishers of truth*, pp. 244–245.
7 *Journal*, ed. Nickalls, p. 132.
8 David M. Butler, *The Quaker meeting houses of Britain*, Vol. 1, p. 349.
9 *Journal*, ed. Nickalls, p. 141.
10 Testimony as preface to Richard Hubberthorne, *A collection of the several books and writings*.
11 *The life & death, travels and sufferings of Robert Widders*, 1688, p. 13; quoted in Isabel Ross, *Margaret Fell: mother of Quakerism*, p. 331.
12 *Journal*, ed. Nickalls, p. 120.

Chapter 7
1 Jennie Levin, *Living threads*, p. 5.
2 See the website www.quaker-tapestry.co.uk
3 George Fox, *Journal*, ed. Nickalls, p. 112.

4   Eric Rothwell, *The priory church of St Mary and St Michael* [Cartmel].
5   *Journal*, ed. Nickalls, p. 113.

Chapter 8
1   George Fox, *Journal*, ed. Nickalls, p. 114.
2   James Wilson, ed., *The Victoria History of the Counties of England: Lancashire*, vol. 2, p. 355.
3   Quoted by Harper Gaythorpe, in 'Swarthmoor meeting-house, Ulverston' p. 239, from a 1686–7 letter to Thomas Lower.
4   Letter from Fox to Lower, quoted by Gaythorpe, p. 240.
5   *Journal*, ed. Nickalls, p. 116.
6   H. Larry Ingle, *First among Friends*, p. 87.
7   *Journal*, ed. Nickalls, p. 127.
8   *Journal*, ed. Nickalls, p. 115.
9   Michael Mullett, ed., *Early Lancaster Friends*, p. 51.
10 Margaret Fell, *A brief collection of remarkable passages…*, pp. 208–209.

Chapter 9
1   Michael Mullett, ed., *Early Lancaster Friends*, p. 7.
2   Matthew 5: 34–37.
3   Margaret Fell, *A brief collection of remarkable passages…*, p.8.

Chapter 10
1   Brian C. Awtry, 'Force Forge in the 17th century' p. 110.
2   Bonnelyn Young Kunze, *Margaret Fell and the rise of Quakerism*, pp. 101–128.
3   Norman Penny, ed., *First publishers of truth*, p. 262.
4   David M. Butler, *The Quaker meeting houses of Britain*, vol. 2, pp. 661–662.
5   George Fox, *Journal*, ed. Nickalls, pp. 171–172.
6   Donald Rooksby, *A people to be gathered*, p. 54.
7   Beatrix Potter, *Journal*, p. 280.
8   *First publishers of truth*, p. 37.
9   George Whitehead, *The Christian progress of George Whitehead*, pp. 124–125.

10 *The Quaker meeting houses of Britain*, vol. 1, p. 43.
11 *First publishers of truth*, p. 52.

Chapter 11
1 *Quaker faith & practice* 20.31; also quoted in Isabel Ross, *Margaret Fell: mother of Quakerism*, p. 380.
2 George Fox, *Journal*, 1694 edition, p. 423.

14

Bibliography

Awtry, Brian C. 'Force Forge in the 17th century', *Transactions of the Cumbria & Westmorland Antiquary and Archaeological Society*, n.s. 77 (1977), 99–112.

Barbour, Hugh. *The Quakers in Puritan England*. New Haven: Yale University Press, 1964.

Besse, Joseph. *Sufferings of early Quakers: Westmorland 1651 to 1690, Cumberland 1653–1690, Durham & Northumberland 1658 to 1690, Isle of Man 1656 to 1685, Lancashire 1652 to 1690*; facsimile of part of the 1753 edition York: Sessions Book Trust, 2000.

Besse, Joseph. *Sufferings of early Quakers: Yorkshire*; facsimile of part of the 1753 edition. York: Sessions Book Trust, 2001.

Boulton, David. *Early Friends in Dent*. Sedbergh: Dales Historical Monographs, 1986.

Boulton, David and Anthea. *In Fox's footsteps*. Dent: Dales Historical Monographs, 1998, revised 2006.

Braithwaite, William C. *The beginnings of Quakerism to 1660*. York: Sessions, 1981 (first published 1912; reprint of 2nd edition 1955).

Butler, David M. *The Quaker meeting houses of Britain*, 2 vols. London: Friends Historical Society, 1999.

Camden, William. *Britannia*; edited and introduced by Robert Mayhew. Bristol: Thoemmes, 2003 (facsimile of 1610 edition).

Damrosch, Leo. *The sorrows of the Quaker Jesus*. Cambridge (MA): Harvard University Press, 1996.

Defoe, Daniel. *A tour through the whole island of Great Britain*, Harmondsworth: Penguin, 1971. (First published 1753).

Eliot, T. S. *The complete poems and plays, 1909–1950*. London: Faber, 1963.

Ellwood, Thomas. *The history of the life of Thomas Ellwood written by himself*; edited and introduced by Rosemary Moore. Walnut Creek, CA, and Oxford: Altamira Press, 2004.

Fell, Margaret. *A brief collection of remarkable passages and occurrences relating to . . . Margaret Fell*. London: J. Sowle, 1710.

The first publishers of truth, ed. Penney, Norman. London: Headley Brothers, 1907. There are versions of this online.

Fox, George. *A journal or historical account of the life, travels, sufferings, Christian experiences and labour of love in the work of the ministry of that ancient, eminent and faithful servant of Jesus*

Christ, George Fox. Thomas Ellwood, ed. London: Thomas Northcott, 1694. The original edition of the *Journal*.

Fox, George. *The journal of George Fox*, rev. ed. by John L. Nickalls. Cambridge University Press, 1952; rev. reprint London: Religious Society of Friends, 1975; and Philadelphia, Philadelphia Yearly Meeting, 1985.

Gaythorpe, Harper. 'Swarthmoor meeting-house, Ulverston: a Quaker stronghold', *Transactions of the Cumbria and Westmorland Antiquarian and Archaeological Society*, n.s. 6 (1906), 237–83.

Hill, Christopher. *The world turned upside down*. London: Penguin, 1991.

Hubberthorne, Richard. *A collection of the several books and writings of that faithful servant of God, Richard Hubberthorne*. London: William Warwick, 1663.

Hyde, Matthew and Nikolaus Pevsner. *Cumbria*. New Haven: Yale University Press, 2010.

Ingle, H. Larry. *First among Friends: George Fox and the creation of Quakerism*. New York: Oxford University Press, 1994.

Kunze, Bonnelyn Young. *Margaret Fell and the rise of Quakerism*. London: Macmillan, 1994.

Levin, Jennie. *Living threads*. Kendal: Quaker Tapestry at Kendal, 1999.

The life & death, travels and sufferings of Robert Widders of Kellet in Lancashire. London: no publisher, 1688.

Machell, Thomas. *Antiquary on horseback*. Jane Ewbank, ed.. Kendal: *Cumberland and Westmorland Antiquary and Archaeological Society*, extra series, vol. 19 (1963).

Marshall, J. D. *Old Lakeland*. Newton Abbot: David and Charles, 1971.

Morgan, Nicholas. *Lancashire Quakers and the establishment 1760–1830*. Halifax: Ryburn, 1993.

Mullett, Michael, ed. *Early Lancaster Friends*. Lancaster: University of Lancaster Press, 1978.

Mullett, Michael A. *Radical religious movements in early modern Europe*. London: Allen & Unwin, 1980.

Neelon, David. *James Nayler: revolutionary to prophet*. Becket, MA: Leadings Press, 2009.

Oxford Dictionary of National Biography. www.oxforddnb.com

Potter, Beatrix. *Journal*, abridged by Glen Cavalero. London: Frederick Warne, 1986.

Punshon, John. *Portrait in grey*, 2nd ed. London: Quaker Books, 2006.

Quaker faith and practice, 4th ed. London: Yearly Meeting of the Religious Society of Friends, 2009.

Reay, Barry. *The Quakers and the English revolution*. London: Temple Smith, 1985.

Rooksby, Donald A. *The Quakers in north-west England*, part 1, *The man in leather breeches*; part 2, *A people to be gathered*; part 3, *And sometime upon the hills*. Colwyn Bay: Donald A. Rooksby, 1994, 1995 and 1998.

Ross, Isabel. *Margaret Fell: mother of Quakerism*. London: Longmans, 1949.

Rothwell, Eric. *The priory church of St Mary and St Michael* [Cartmel]. Much Wenlock: R.H. Smith, 2000.

Rowntree, John Wilhelm. *Essays and addresses*. Joshua Rowntree, ed. London: Headley Bros., 1905.

Stephenson, Roy, '1652 Country: a land steeped in our faith', *The Friend* (8 Oct. 2010), 10–12.

Victoria history of the county of Cumberland. James Wilson, ed., vol. 2. London: James Street, 1905.

The Victoria history of the counties of England: Lancashire, vols. 7 and 8. London: Constable, 1912 and 1914.

Whitehead, George. *The Christian progress of George Whitehead*. London: J. Sowle, 1725.

Whittaker, E. Jean. *Thomas Lawson 1630–1691*. York: Sessions, 1986.

Winchester, Angus. *The 1652 Country*. N.p.: North West 1652 Committee, 2010.

Woolman, John. *The journal and major essays*, New York: OUP, 1971; reprinted Richmond, Indiana: Friends United Press, 1989.

Wordsworth, William. *Poetical works*. Thomas Hutchinson and rev. Ernest de Selincourt, eds. London: Oxford University Press, 1965.